D1538658

Social Issues
in Literature

Class Conflict
in Charles Dickens's
A Tale of Two Cities

Other Books in the Social Issues in Literature Series:

Social Issues in Literature

Class Conflict in Charles Dickens's *A Tale of Two Cities*

Dedria Bryfonski, Book Editor

GREENHAVEN PRESS
A part of Gale, Cengage Learning

GALE
CENGAGE Learning·

Detroit • New York • San Francisco • New Haven, Conn • Waterville, Maine • London

Elizabeth Des Chenes, *Director, Content Strategy*
Cynthia Sanner, *Publisher*
Douglas Dentino, *Manager, New Product*

For more information, contact:
Greenhaven Press
27500 Drake Rd.
Farmington Hills, MI 48331-3535
Or you can visit our Internet site at gale.cengage.com

For product information and technology assistance, contact us at

Gale Customer Support, 1-800-877-4253
For permission to use material from this text or product, submit all requests online at www.cengage.com/permissions

Further permissions questions can be emailed to permissionrequest@cengage.com

Articles in Greenhaven Press anthologies are often edited for length to meet page requirements. In addition, original titles of these works are changed to clearly present the main thesis and to explicitly indicate the author's opinion. Every effort is made to ensure that Greenhaven Press accurately reflects the original intent of the authors. Every effort has been made to trace the owners of copyrighted material.

Cover image © World History Archive/Alamy.

LIBRARY OF CONGRESS CATALOGING-IN-PUBLICATION DATA

Class conflict in Charles Dickens's A tale of two cities / Dedria Bryfonski, Book Editor.
    pages cm. -- (Social Issues in Literature)
    Includes bibliographical references and index.
    ISBN 978-0-7377-6974-6 (hardcover) -- ISBN 978-0-7377-6975-3 (pbk.)
    1. Dickens, Charles, 1812-1870. Tale of two cities. 2. Social conflict in literature.
3. Bryfonski, Dedria, editor of compilation.
    PR4571.C56 2013
    823'.8--dc23
                                                                    2013004128

Printed in Mexico
1 2 3 4 5 6 7 17 16 15 14 13

Contents

Although in *A Tale of Two Cities* Dickens is unrelenting in his condemnation of the oppression of the common people by the French aristocracy, he is equally critical of the mayhem unleashed by the revolutionary mob.

A *Tale of Two Cities* reflects Dickens's uneasiness with both French and English society. The aristocracy in France is shown as exploiting both peasants and the urban middle class. In England, the situation is more complex, with some professions, such as the law, enjoying more autonomy than others.

Chapter 3: Contemporary Perspectives on Class Conflict

Concerns that income inequality has increased and represents a significant problem in America are overstated and misleading. Instead of focusing on income inequality, legislators should focus on fixing the educational system, which is the surest method of achieving equality of opportunity.

Between 1984 and 2009, the only group whose median net worth increased was those fifty-five and older. Despite this, America has a system that taxes younger people to fund entitlements, such as Medicare and Social Security, which benefit older people who are much better off financially.

Introduction

Virtually any listing of the top novelists of all time will include Charles Dickens. He was an author who enjoyed popular success during his lifetime and whose works continue to be part of classroom curriculums and read for enjoyment. More than two hundred million copies of his *A Tale of Two Cities* have been sold, making it the best-selling novel of all time. Factors contributing to the enduring popularity of Dickens are his memorable characterizations, compelling story lines, descriptive powers, and strong themes of social justice.

Dickens was the second child and first son of John and Elizabeth Dickens, who would have eight children altogether. By all accounts, Dickens had a very happy childhood up to the age of twelve, most of it spent in a prosperous neighborhood in Chatham. However, John Dickens, an assistant clerk in the navy pay office, lived beyond his means. He was transferred to London in 1822. Because family finances were becoming strapped, the family was compelled to take up residence in Camden Town, a lower-middle-class part of London. John Dickens's poor money management resulted in a sentence at Marshalsea prison, a debtors' prison, in February 1824. His wife and younger children joined him, leaving the two older children in London. Charles Dickens's sister Fanny was a talented musician studying at the Royal Academy of Music, and she was allowed to stay there. Young Charles, however, was sent out to work to help the family finances. A family friend secured employment for Dickens pasting labels on bottles at Warren's Blacking Factory. Lodging was found for Dickens at two successive boarding houses, but he was essentially left to fend for himself at the age of twelve. In June 1824, John Dickens received an inheritance from his grandmother, and the Dickens family left prison and returned to London. Within a few months, Dickens was permitted to stop work at the blacking factory and resume his schooling, but the memory of those wretched days had a profound effect on the man and writer. He kept quiet about the experience, later telling only his wife, Catherine, and his friend and biographer John Forster. Forster quotes Dickens in the biography *The Life of Charles Dickens*:

> "No words can express the secret agony of my soul as I sunk into this companionship [of 'common men and boys'] . . . and felt my early hopes of growing up to be a learned and distinguished man, crushed in my breast. The deep remembrance of the sense I had of being utterly neglected and hopeless; of the shame I felt in my position; of the misery it was to my young heart to believe that, day by day, what I had learned, and thought, and delighted in, and raised my fancy and my emulation up by, was passing away from me, never to be brought back any more; cannot be written."

This firsthand experience of wretched poverty, loneliness, and class politics is credited with awakening in Dickens an abiding concern with class injustice, an issue that would make him an ardent social crusader. Class conflict is a recurring theme in Dickens's work and is central to *A Tale of Two Cities*, with the French Revolution being the ultimate in class struggles.

A Tale of Two Cities is an unusual work in the Dickens canon—it is one of only two historic novels, and it lacks the brilliant characterizations and highly descriptive writing style of his other works. Several critics suggest that Dickens selected the French Revolution as his subject matter as an analogy for the turmoil that was occurring in his own life at the time. Dickens wrote *A Tale of Two Cities* from 1857–59. For many years, Charles and Catherine's marriage had been an unhappy one. During the final years of their living together, he moved into a separate bedroom and had the door adjoining his wife's bedroom boarded up. While acting in *The Frozen Deep* in the summer of 1857, Dickens met and fell in love with an eighteen-year-old actress, Ellen Ternan. According to contemporary accounts, a bracelet intended for Ternan was delivered by mistake to Dickens's wife, precipitating a final breakdown of the marriage. Dickens secured a legal separation from his wife in 1858 and set up Ternan and her family members in a house. Reacting to rumors, Dickens wrote a statement about his personal affairs that appeared in the *Times*. When his publisher, Bradbury and Evans, refused to publish the statement in its periodical *Punch*, Dickens severed his publishing relationship and returned to his former publisher, Chapman & Hall. Rumors of his personal affairs also led to a falling out with several of his friends, including novelist William Makepeace Thackeray.

Critic Jack Lindsay, writing in *Life and Letters* in September 1949, suggests that Dickens used the French Revolution as a vehicle to confront his own personal crises:

> "*A Tale of Two Cities* is built up from the episode of Dr. Manette's unjust imprisonment; and its whole working-out is concerned with the effects of that unjust deprivation of light and joy: effects which entangle everyone round the Doctor and recoil back on his own head in unpredictable ways. The Doctor's fate is thus for Dickens both a symbol of the Revolution, its deeds, causes, and consequences, and of himself, immured in a maddening cell of lies and cruelties, and seeking to break through into the truth, into a full and happy relationship with his fellows. It was the demented sense of environing pressures, of an unjust inescapable mechanism, which caught Dickens up in the midst of his wild mummery and gave him a sense of release when he determined to write the novel. . . ."

> "In this dire tangle of moral consequences we see Dickens confronting his own confused situation and trying to equate his own moment of painful compelled choice with the revolutionary moment in which a definite break is made with the old, amid violent birth pangs, and makes possible the rebirth of life, the renewal of love and innocence."

The essays in *Social Issues in Literature: Class Conflict in Charles Dickens's A Tale of Two Cities* examine class conflict in the novel as well as its manifestations in contemporary society.

Chronology

1812

Charles Dickens is born on February 7 in Landport, Hampshire. He is the second child and first son of John and Elizabeth Barrow Dickens.

1814

The Dickens family moves to London where John Dickens is a clerk in the navy pay office.

1816

The Dickens family moves to Chatham, Kent, where Charles Dickens attends William Giles's school.

1822

The Dickens family moves to Camden Town, a poor section of London.

1824

John Dickens is imprisoned from February 2 to May 28 in the Marshalsea prison for debt. The rest of the Dickens family accompanies him to Marshalsea, leaving Charles Dickens to live alone in Camden Town and work at Warren's Blacking Factory. John comes into an inheritance and is released from prison. The family returns to Camden Town, and Dickens attends Wellington Academy in the fall.

1827

Dickens leaves school and is employed as a solicitor's clerk.

1830

Dickens begins reading literature and history at the British Museum library. He learns shorthand and becomes a court stenographer. He falls in love with Maria Beadnell, the daughter of a successful banker.

1832

The parents of Maria Beadnell send her abroad, succeeding in their desire to break off her relationship with Dickens.

1834

Dickens's first sketch, *A Dinner at Poplar Walk*, is published in the January issue of *Monthly Magazine*. He becomes a news reporter for the *Morning Chronicle*. John Dickens is once again arrested for debt, and Charles Dickens comes to his aid.

1836

Sketches by Boz is published. *The Posthumous Papers of the Pickwick Club*, also known as *The Pickwick Papers*, begins publication as a monthly serial. Dickens marries Catherine Hogarth, the daughter of the editor of the *Morning Chronicle*, on April 2. Dickens becomes editor of *Bentley's Miscellany*.

1837

Oliver Twist begins publication as a monthly serial in *Bentley's Miscellany*. *The Posthumous Papers of the Pickwick Club* is published as Dickens's first novel. Charles Jr., the first of ten children of Dickens and his wife, is born.

1838

Nicholas Nickleby begins publication as a monthly serial. *Oliver Twist* is published as a novel. Daughter Mary is born.

1839

A second daughter, Kate, is born. Dickens resigns as editor of *Bentley's Miscellany*. *Nicholas Nickleby* is published as a novel.

1840

The Old Curiosity Shop is serialized in *Master Humphrey's Clock*, a weekly journal.

1841

Barnaby Rudge: A Tale of the Riots of 'Eighty is published. *The Old Curiosity Shop* is published as a novel. A son, Walter, is born.

1842

Dickens and his wife tour the United States and Canada from January until June. *American Notes* is published.

1843

The Life and Adventures of Martin Chuzzlewit begins publication as a monthly serial. *A Christmas Carol* is published.

1844

Dickens tours Italy with his family. They return to London in December when *The Chimes* is published. Dickens travels to Genoa, Italy. *The Life and Adventures of Martin Chuzzlewit* is published as a novel. A fifth child, Francis, is born.

1845

Dickens's amateur theatrical company debuts. He returns to England in July. A sixth child, Alfred, is born. *The Cricket on the Hearth* is published.

1846

Pictures from Italy and *The Battle of Life* are published, and *Dombey and Son* begins publication as a monthly serial. Dickens travels to Switzerland in May.

1847

Dickens lives in Lausanne, Switzerland, and then Paris. A seventh child, Sydney, is born.

1848

The novella *The Haunted Man* is published. *Dombey and Son* is published as a novel.

1849

David Copperfield begins publication as a monthly serial. An eighth child, Henry, is born.

1850

Dickens establishes a new weekly journal, *Household Words.* *David Copperfield* is published as a novel. A third daughter, Dora, is born.

1851

Dickens visits Paris. *A Child's History of England* begins publication in *Household Words.* Dora dies.

1852

Bleak House begins publication as a monthly serial. *A Child's History of England* begins publication in book form. A final child, Edward, is born.

1853

Dickens tours Italy and Switzerland. *Bleak House* is published as a novel.

1854

Hard Times begins publication as a monthly serial in *Household Words* in April. It is published as a novel in August.

1855

Little Dorrit begins publication as a monthly serial. Dickens visits Paris.

1856

Dickens buys Gad's Hill Place in Kent.

1857

Dickens acts in Wilkie Collins's play *The Frozen Deep* and meets and falls in love with actress Ellen Ternan. *Little Dorrit* is published as a novel.

1858

Dickens and his wife legally separate. He engages in a series of public readings.

1859

Dickens establishes a new journal, *All the Year Round*, and *A Tale of Two Cities* is serialized in it. Later that year, *A Tale of Two Cities* is published as a novel.

1860

The Uncommercial Traveller and *Great Expectations* begin serialization in *All the Year Round*. Dickens holds a second round of public readings.

1861

Great Expectations is published as a novel.

1864

Our Mutual Friend begins publication as a monthly serial.

1865

Our Mutual Friend, which will be Dickens's last complete novel, is published.

1866

Dickens holds a third series of public readings.

1867

Dickens goes on a reading tour of the United States.

1868

Dickens begins a farewell reading tour.

1869

The reading tour is curtailed due to Dickens's failing health.

1870

Dickens begins his final work, *The Mystery of Edwin Drood*. He dies on June 9 and is buried in Westminster Abbey on June 14.

Background on
Charles Dickens

The Life of Charles Dickens

George H. Ford

George H. Ford was an internationally recognized Dickens scholar and a former chair of the English Department at the University of Rochester. He was a founding editor of the Norton Anthology of English Literature *and the author of* Dickens and His Readers.

Unlike many authors whose genius is not recognized during their lifetimes, Charles Dickens became a critically acclaimed and prosperous writer at an early age, states Ford in the following viewpoint. A possible reason for Dickens's driving ambition, the critic speculates, was his early hardship and rejection by his first love. As Dickens aged, his writing continued to develop, with masterpieces such as Great Expectations *written toward the end of his life, Ford explains.*

The life story of Charles Dickens is, from several perspectives, a success story. Generally regarded today as one of the greatest novelists in the English language, Dickens had the unusual good fortune to have been recognized by his contemporaries as well as by posterity. He was not one of the neglected artists such as [John] Keats, doomed to wait for later generations to discover his stature. Instead, Dickens's *The Posthumous Papers of the Pickwick Club* (1836–1837), which began publication when he was twenty-four years old, was a phenomenally popular success on both sides of the Atlantic. Before he was thirty, when he had already produced five vastly scaled novels, he came to America for a visit and was accorded the most triumphant reception ever staged for a foreign visitor. As the newspapers said, even the enthusiastic re-

George H. Ford, "Charles Dickens," *Victorian Novelists Before 1885*, ed. Matthew Joseph Bruccoli, 0E. © 1984 Cengage Learning.

ception of General Lafayette [a French military officer who was a major general in the American Revolutionary War] in 1824 did not equal the way Dickens was received. His success was also reflected in his earnings: In the 1850s Dickens was making as much as £11,000 for one of his novels, a figure to be contrasted with the mere £600 earned in a year by his eminent contemporary and fellow novelist [William Makepeace] Thackeray. After his death the success story continued. . . .

Happiness and Hardship

In the history of novel writing, Dickens's early start stands out as especially unusual. Poets and musicians often create significant compositions in their youth. Novelists, contrariwise (at least major novelists), are generally late starters, perhaps because novel writing calls for perspectives of a special sort. The explanation for Dickens's early start is provided by the all-purpose word *genius,* with which the young man was evidently abundantly endowed. But genius in novel writing needs experiences to work with, painful experiences as well as pleasant ones. It was Dickens's fortune to have encountered both sorts while still a youth. Dickens's ancestry included a mixture of servants and office workers. His paternal grandfather, who died before Dickens was born, had been a steward in an aristocratic estate where Dickens's grandmother (who died when the boy was twelve) had been the housekeeper. One of her two sons, John Dickens (1785–1851), who had grown up on this country estate, obtained employment in London at the pay office of the British navy, a position that necessitated his moving to other localities from time to time. John Dickens was to be immortalized many years later by his son's portrait of him as Mr. Micawber [in the novel *David Copperfield*]. He reputedly resembled Micawber in loquaciousness and in pseudoelegance of manner, as well as in his fondness for libations—all of which make him sound like the father of another literary genius, James Joyce. In 1809 John Dickens married

Elizabeth Barrow (1789–1863), whose father also worked in the pay office. Years later, she, too, would be the model for one of her son's characters, the fast-chattering Mrs. Nickleby [in the novel *Nicholas Nickleby*]. With two such talkers for parents, the son was to have a more than adequate early exposure to the spoken voice.

Eight children were born to John and Elizabeth, the first, Frances (Fanny), in 1810, and the second, Charles, over a year later. His birthplace was a house in Portsmouth, a town to which his father had been transferred some time previously. Except for a short stay in London, Dickens's boyhood was passed in towns on the south coast of England, especially in the twin towns of Rochester and Chatham, where the family settled when he was five. This pocket of preindustrial England had a powerful impact on Dickens's attitudes. He is conventionally thought of as the novelist of the big city, which he was; but it is noteworthy that during the last ten years of his life he chose to live not in London but near the town of Rochester, in Kent, in the region where he had spent his boyhood. Here in the town of Chatham he had attended a good school; discovered his favorite novelists, such as [Tobias] Smollett; and generally enjoyed himself. He did suffer from bouts of ill health; and sometimes he was afraid to go to bed after listening to the hair-raising bedtime stories inflicted on him by the nurse, especially a story called "Captain Murderer." Nevertheless, these first eleven years were happy ones.

This idyll was shattered after his family moved to London, where his father's casual mismanagement of his income finally led to his imprisonment for debt and to his twelve-year-old son's being sent to work in a blacking warehouse. The boy's job consisted of pasting labels on bottles of black shoe polish, this menial job being performed near a window within sight of passersby in the street. Living alone in cheap lodgings and nearly starving, Charles was overwhelmed with a sense of having been willfully abandoned by his parents and sentenced to remain in a rat hole for life. That his novels would be full of characters who are orphans is not surprising. The blacking warehouse experience lasted in reality only a few months, but to the boy, and to the grown man in retrospect, the time seemed endless. As he wrote in his autobiography more than twenty years later: "I never had the courage to go back to the place where my servitude began. . . . My old way home by the borough made me cry, after my eldest child could speak." Eventually he was rescued by his father, who had acquired some funds, and was sent to a school in London from the ages of twelve to fifteen. His mother, strangely unaware of her son's feelings, wanted him to stay at work rather than resume school, and Dickens never forgave her for her failure to provide the love and understanding he most desperately needed. . . .

Insecurity and Ambition

The importance of these unhappy experiences, especially in a career so seemingly happy and successful, cannot be exaggerated; it set up in Dickens's mind a specter of insecurity that was never to disappear. These experiences may also have contributed to his zealous resolution to excel and to his almost ruthless energy in all his pursuits, in particular his writing. As he noted in a letter of 1855: "Whoever is devoted to an art must be content to deliver himself wholly up to it, and to find his recompense in it." Dickens has often been characterized as the great recorder of life in the Victorian age, or as one of its major critics, but he was also, in his energetic pursuit of his goals, the embodiment of his age, the archetypal Victorian.

With the dark world behind him, Dickens began attending school at Wellington Academy in London. It was not as good a school as the one he had attended in Chatham, but it served his purposes, and at the end of his three years there he was head of his class and the winner of a prize for Latin. At fifteen he had finished his formal education and begun a lifetime of

Charles Dickens (1812–1870) was an English writer and social critic. Some consider him to be the greatest novelist of Victorian England. © FPG/Lifesize/Getty Images.

work. The possibility that he might go on to a university was apparently never considered by anyone. One of Dickens's sons, Henry, would attend Cambridge, but he himself was to acquire learning on his own; his college was the great library of the British Museum in London, where he was admitted as a reader on his eighteenth birthday. Here he soaked himself in works of history and literature (especially [playwright William] Shakespeare) that would make up a storehouse of knowledge to draw upon during the busy years ahead. In sum, Dickens's education, formal and informal, did not equip him to edit a learned journal such as the *Westminster Review* (of which George Eliot, the most erudite of novelists, would be an editor), but it did equip him to write novels. Perhaps a more extensive exposure to learning would have enabled him to write a better version of his embarrassingly crude potboiler *A Child's History of England* (1852–1854), but it is doubtful that it would have enabled him to write a better novel than the one he was writing at the same time, his great masterpiece *Bleak House* (1852–1853).

During the seven years after leaving school, the young Dickens lived at home with his family (although he was sometimes absent on trips). His experience during this apprentice period included exposure to the worlds of law, politics, journalism, and the theater. For the first two years he was a clerk in a law office, and it is remarkable how often in his novels he sets up scenes, usually comic ones, portraying the antics of junior clerks in lawyers' offices. For the next four years his employment involved the preparation of shorthand reports for lawyers who worked in Doctors' Commons. He had learned shorthand from one of his uncles, John Henry Barrow, an experienced reporter, who eventually obtained for Dickens a position as shorthand reporter in Parliament. Dickens's mastery of shorthand gained him some notoriety both for his speed and his accuracy, and these skills continued to be of use to him in his next position, that of a news reporter on the staff of the *Morning Chronicle*, which he joined in 1834. In this new role, he was frequently sent on journeys to report on election speeches in distant places. From his two years as a reporter of political events as well as from his years covering

Parliament, Dickens acquired an extraordinary amount of information about the political life of his country during a crucial period following the passing of the Reform Bill of 1832. He also acquired from these experiences a realization that political oratory is often absurdly empty. . . .

Love and Rejection

In 1830, Dickens was introduced into the household of George Beadnell, a prosperous banker, and his wife and their three daughters. The youngest daughter, Maria, was twenty years old, and with her the eighteen-year-old Dickens fell overwhelmingly in love. Writing to her three years later, Dickens still affirmed: "I never have loved and I never can love any human creature breathing but yourself." The relationship developed happily for some time, and at the outset, Maria was apparently encouraging with her teenaged suitor. But by 1832, her parents began to discourage his attentions, perhaps having heard reports about his father's unreliability, or perhaps on the grounds that Dickens himself did not seem to have suitable prospects. In any event, Maria was sent abroad to a finishing school in Paris, and after her return, her interest in Dickens had cooled altogether. In March 1833, he returned all the letters she had written to him, lamenting his fate and reminding her, with a flourish, that she had been "the object of my first, and my last love." The infatuation lasted four years, and the frustrations of the relationship were even more painful for Dickens to look back upon than were his experiences in the blacking warehouse. . . .

One of the lasting effects of the thwarting was its influence on his desire to succeed and to become financially secure, just as David Copperfield, in his novel, would be impelled to strenuous efforts to succeed. As Dickens explained to [his friend and biographer John] Forster: "I went at it with a determination to overcome all the difficulties, which fairly lifted me up into that newspaper life, and floated me away over a hundred men's heads." When at last Dickens tried his hand at literature, the same driving energies persisted: with his pen he would show those unseeing banking Beadnells (by heaven!) what a paragon they had missed being allied to. But first he had to pass through his literary apprenticeship as he had passed through his earlier apprenticeships to law, journalism, and the stage. During the three years before launching his first full-length novel, Dickens was learning the craft of literature by writing occasional short pieces which he called sketches. Some of these pieces tell a story; others are simply descriptions of London localities such as Newgate Prison or Monmouth Street (the shopping center for secondhand clothing); and others offer portraits of picturesque characters such as a cabdriver or a circus clown.

Early Success

The first sketch, *A Dinner at Poplar Walk*, was submitted for publication in late 1833, when Dickens was twenty-one, and appeared in the *Monthly Magazine*, in January 1834. . . . The emotional satisfaction of seeing his sketch in print was the only reward Dickens received for this publication; indeed, he received no payments whatever for the first nine of his sketches, which were all published in the *Monthly Magazine*. Thereafter, having established his literary credentials, he was able to require payments for his efforts when they appeared in magazines or newspapers and receive further payments when the sketches were collected and published in volumes in 1836. There were some sixty sketches in all, making up two volumes entitled *Sketches by Boz*. . . .

Sketches by Boz was well received by reviewers and had an encouraging sale. . . .

This review [a favorable review], appearing in the *Morning Chronicle* on 11 February 1836, gave Dickens a special degree of pleasure because of its having been written by George Hogarth, his prospective father-in-law. Hogarth (1783–1870) was a cultivated man of many talents. After working some years as a lawyer in Edinburgh, where he had connections with Sir Walter Scott, he gave up law for journalism and moved to England as a newspaper editor. He was also an accomplished musician and the author of books and articles about music. In 1834, he and Dickens came to know each other at the offices of the *Morning Chronicle*, and Dickens was soon a frequent visitor at Hogarth's house, where he met the eldest daughter, Catherine (1815–1879), who was called Kate. George Hogarth was an admirer of the *Sketches by Boz* (as his review indicated), knowing them "by heart," as Dickens remarked. Dickens, in turn, became an admirer of Hogarth's pretty daughter. Early in 1835 he became engaged to her, and in April 1836, they were married. . . .

Serial Publishing

Dickens's shift from being a writer of sketches to a writer of novels was effected in a remarkably haphazard way. A few days after his twenty-fourth birthday in 1836, he received a proposal from Chapman & Hall, who were planning to bring out a book of illustrations by a well-known comic artist, Robert Seymour (1798–1836). What the publishers wanted from Dickens was a series of comic stories and sketches that could provide materials for Seymour to illustrate. The series would eventually appear as a book, but its first appearance would be in twenty monthly installments. Dickens at once set to work, and by late March, within a day of his marriage to Catherine Hogarth, the first installment appeared of *The Posthumous Papers of the Pickwick Club*, later to be known simply as *The Pickwick Papers*. . . .

One important legacy of his having started working with Seymour was the distinctive method of publication in monthly numbers that they had adopted. As a way of publishing novels, this was an innovation, and one that gradually came to be looked upon with favor by the early Victorian reading public.

All of Dickens's novels were to be published in installments; and for thirty-five years or so after *The Pickwick Papers*, other novelists, such as Thackeray, would also publish in monthly numbers. An interesting feature of serial publication was its enabling the novelist to get an early impression of how the work was being received by the public. *The Pickwick Papers* looked at first like a loser: the opening chapters failed to attract attention, and only 500 copies of the second installment were printed. Some months later, the publishers were frantically trying to print enough copies to meet the demands of thousands of *Pickwick Papers* enthusiasts. Of the final number (October 1837), some 40,000 copies were printed. What was the reason for this turnaround? Most of Dickens's contemporaries traced the change to the fourth number, in which he had introduced two strikingly colorful cockney characters: Sam Weller and his father, Tony, the fat coachman. Sam's mixture of impudence and warmheartedness, and his worldly-wise anecdotes purveyed in a lively cockney accent, made him an ideal foil for Mr. Pickwick's innocent and well-intentioned benevolence. By having Sam become Mr. Pickwick's servant, Dickens had recreated an endearing pair like Sancho Panza and Don Quixote [characters in the novel *Don Quixote* by Miguel de Cervantes], and his readers greeted the combination with a level of enthusiasm rarely to be matched in the history of literature. *The Pickwick Papers* ended up as the most sensational triumph in nineteenth-century publishing. . . .

In Demand and Overcommitted

[At] the age of twenty-four, Dickens began to earn enough from his writing of fiction so as to be able to give up working for the *Morning Chronicle*, which he did in November 1836. It was well that he could do so, for at this time he was absurdly overcommitted to a long list of literary projects and deadlines. Sparked by the dizzying success of *The Pickwick Papers* and by a youthful faith that his energy was unfathomable, and also aware of his new responsibilities as husband and father-to-be, Dickens had signed one agreement after another with three different publishers during 1836. The *Sketches by Boz* would be completed, fortunately, in December, but *The Pickwick Papers* was only halfway complete at this date, and an installment had to be written for every month until November 1837. Dickens had also made a loose agreement with another publisher that he would have completed a novel, "Gabriel Vardon," [eventually published as *Barnaby Rudge: A Tale of the Riots of 'Eighty*] by November 1836! . . .

The following year, 1837, was a little less frantic. It opened with the publication of the first of the twenty-four monthly installments of his second novel, *Oliver Twist*. . . . For readers who had grown fondly accustomed to the fun and frolics of successive numbers of *The Pickwick Papers*, this new novel by Boz must have prompted a sense of shock. Most of the adventures of the young protagonist consist of a succession of encounters with the worlds of brutality and crime. . . .

More Critically Acclaimed Works

[Dickens completed] *The Pickwick Papers* late in 1837 and *Oliver Twist* in spring 1839; and then, before he was thirty, he published three more full-length novels: *Nicholas Nickleby*, *The Old Curiosity Shop*, and *Barnaby Rudge*. It was an extraordinary performance, and all of these novels were (*Barnaby Rudge* less so) popular and critical successes. . . .

[The principal efforts of the last two decades of Dickens's life] were expended on the writing of novels. Following the final number of *Dombey and Son* there was a rest period of about a year before the fresh and delightful opening number of *The Personal History of David Copperfield* was published in May 1849. It was an immediate hit, and after seven months, Dickens could report in a letter: "I think it is better liked than any of my other books." . . .

If satirical exposures of institutional inadequacies were kept to the minimum in *David Copperfield*, Dickens seems to have decided to make up for his restraint when he began writing his next novel, *Bleak House*. This work seethes with discontents sometimes expressed in fiery invectives, discontents which are also prominent in others of his novels of the 1850s and 1860s: *Hard Times* (1854), *Little Dorrit*, and *Our Mutual Friend* (1864–1865). This group, anticipated by *Dombey and Son*, was labeled by Lionel Stevenson as Dickens's "Dark Period" novels, and the term seems apt. . . .

A New Home, and a Separation

The financial rewards from *Little Dorrit* and from *Household Words* enabled Dickens, as he was finishing the novel, to realize a dream of his early boyhood. Gad's Hill Place, a beautiful eighteenth-century brick house on a hill outside of Rochester, which he had admired during walks with his father, came up for sale, and he bought it. . . . It had plenty of room for guests (it is today a boarding school for girls), attractive gardens, and a surrounding landscape ideal for walks. Dickens lived there for the final ten years of his life (he sold Tavistock House [where he lived with his family beginning in 1851] in 1860). This happy realization of a boyhood dream coincided with an opposite kind of development: the gradual breaking up of his marriage, culminating in a legal separation from Kate in May 1858.

Hints of his growing dissatisfaction as a husband can be detected in his letters of the early 1850s in references to his "miserable" marriage, and in his report to Forster: "Poor Catherine and I are not made for each other, and there is no help for it." But the formal break did not occur until Dickens had met an attractive eighteen-year-old actress, Ellen Ternan, who eventually became his mistress. . . .

[In] 1858, incidents involving the Ellen Ternan story led to a quarrel between Dickens and his publishers Bradbury and

Evans and to his starting a new periodical to replace *House-hold Words*. Published by Chapman & Hall, *All the Year Round* was another success with the reading public, reaching a circulation of 100,000 in the 1860s. Part of its success is attributable to Dickens's publishing in its pages two of his best-known novels: *A Tale of Two Cities* (1859) and *Great Expectations* (1861). The first of these has been one of his most popular novels, especially in the United States, where, in 1970, more copies were sold than of any other novel by Dickens. . . .

At the time of Dickens's changing his publishers, his career underwent another and more important change: In April 1858, he finally decided, after much hesitation, to start a tour during which he would do readings from his own writings, such as *A Christmas Carol* and the trial scene in *The Pickwick Papers*. At this date he was already an experienced and highly successful reader, but heretofore his performances had been to raise money for charities. Now, instead, he was starred as a professional, raising money for himself. Yet it is evident that he took on this new career not just to earn money; he needed the direct contact with vast audiences of his readers in order to compensate for a sense of loneliness and dissatisfaction which afflicted him powerfully in these late years. The readings exhausted him (his first tour called for eighty-seven performances), but they also exhilarated him. . . .

A Writer for the Ages

The last completed page of *The Mystery of Edwin Drood* was written at Gad's Hill on the afternoon of 8 June 1870. That evening Dickens was stricken with an aneurysm in the brain and died the following day without regaining consciousness. Even though he had wanted to be buried in the Rochester area which was so deeply associated with both his lost childhood and with recent triumphs and losses, his wish had to be overruled in favor of Westminster Abbey. On 14 June, in a private ceremony, he was buried in Poets' Corner, which the *Times* described on this occasion as "the peculiar resting place of English literary genius."

Dickens Was Skilled at Character Development

Mamie Dickens

Mary "Mamie" Dickens was the oldest daughter of Charles Dickens. In addition to writing My Father as I Recall Him, *a collection of reminiscences, she was also the coeditor of* The Letters of Charles Dickens.

Charles Dickens was a genius at character development because he felt so deeply about his characters, declares his daughter in the following viewpoint. Writing about the short life and early death of the character Nell Trent from The Old Curiosity Shop *was deeply disturbing to Dickens, his daughter relates. She points out that her father was equally skilled at creating admirable and despicable characters.*

When at work my father was almost always alone, so that, with rare exceptions, save as we could see the effect of the adventures of his characters upon him in his daily moods, we knew but little of his manner of work. Absolute quiet under these circumstances was essential, the slightest sound making an interruption fatal to the success of his labors, although, oddly enough, in his leisure hours the bustle and noise of a great city seemed necessary to him. . . .

As I have said, he was usually alone when at work, though there were, of course, some occasional exceptions, and I myself constituted such an exception. During our life at Tavistock House, I had a long and serious illness, with an almost equally long convalescence. During the latter, my father suggested that I should be carried every day into his study to remain with him, and, although I was fearful of disturbing him, he assured

Mamie Dickens, "At His Work," *My Father as I Recall Him*, E.P. Dutton and Co., 1896, pp. 46–68.

me that he desired to have me with him. On one of these mornings, I was lying on the sofa endeavouring to keep perfectly quiet, while my father wrote busily and rapidly at his desk, when he suddenly jumped from his chair and rushed to a mirror which hung near, and in which I could see the reflection of some extraordinary facial contortions which he was making. He returned rapidly to his desk, wrote furiously for a few moments, and then went again to the mirror. The facial pantomime was resumed, and then turning toward, but evidently not seeing, me, he began talking rapidly in a low voice. Ceasing this soon, however, he returned once more to his desk, where he remained silently writing until luncheon time. It was a most curious experience for me, and one of which, I did not until later years, fully appreciate the purport. Then I knew that with his natural intensity he had thrown himself completely into the character that he was creating, and that for the time being he had not only lost sight of his surroundings, but had actually become in action, as in imagination, the creature of his pen. . . .

Dickens Suffered with His Characters

That he was always in earnest, that he lived with his creations, that their joys and sorrows were his joys and sorrows, that at times his anguish, both of body and spirit, was poignant and heartbreaking, I know. His interest in and love for his characters were intense as his nature, and is shown nowhere more strongly than in his sufferings during his portrayal of the short life of "Little Nell," like a father he mourned for his little girl—the child of his brain—and he writes: "I am, for the time, nearly dead with work and grief for the loss of my child." Again he writes of her: "You can't imagine (gravely I write and speak) how exhausted I am today with yesterday's labors. I went to bed last night utterly dispirited and done up. All night I have been pursued by the child; and this morning I am unrefreshed and miserable. I do not know what to do with myself."

His love and care for this little one are shown most pathetically in the suggestions which he gave to Mr. George Cattermole [an English painter] for his illustrations of *The Old Curiosity Shop*. "Kit, the single gentleman, and Mr. Garland go down to the place where the child is and arrive there at night. There has been a fall of snow. Kit, leaving them behind, runs to the old house, and with a lantern in one hand, and the bird in its cage in the other, stops for a moment at a little distance, with a natural hesitation, before he goes up to make his presence known. In a window—supposed to be that of the child's little room—a light is burning, and in that room the child (unknown, of course, to her visitors, who are full of hope), lies dead."

Again: "The child lying dead in the little sleeping room, behind the open screen. It is winter time, so there are no flowers, but upon her breast and pillow there may be strips of holly and berries and such green things. A window, overgrown with ivy. The little boy who had that talk with her about the angels may be by the bedside, if you like it so; but I think it will be quieter and more peaceful if she is quite alone. I want the scene to express the most beautiful repose and tranquillity, and to have something of a happy look, if death can do this."

Another: "The child has been buried within the church, and the old man, who cannot be made to understand that she is dead repairs to the grave and sits there all day long, waiting for her arrival to begin another journey. His staff and knapsack, her little bonnet and basket, lie beside him. 'She'll come to-morrow,' he says, when it gets dark, and then goes sorrowfully home. I think an hour glass running out would keep up the notion; perhaps her little things upon his knee or in his hand. I am breaking my heart over this story, and cannot bear to finish it."

In acknowledging the receipt of a letter concerning this book from Mr. John Tomlin, an American, he wrote: "I thank you cordially and heartily for your letter, and for its kind and

An illustration of the Dickens characters Nell Trent and her grandfather from The Old Curiosity Shop, *published in 1840.* © William Holman Hunt/The Bridgeman Art Library/ Getty Images.

courteous terms. To think that I have awakened among the vast solitudes in which you dwell a fellow feeling and sympathy with the creatures of many thoughtful hours, is the source of the purest delight and pride to me; and believe me that your expressions of affectionate remembrance and approval, sounding from the green forests of the Mississippi, sink deeper into my heart and gratify it more than all the honorary distinctions that all the courts of Europe could confer. It is such things as these that make one hope one does not live in vain, and that are the highest rewards of an author's life."

Dickens Made His Characters Come to Life

His genius for character sketching needs no proof—his characters live to vouch for themselves, for their reality. It is ever amazing to me that the hand which drew the pathetic and beautiful creations, the kindly humored men, the lovely women, the unfortunate little ones, could portray also with such marvellous accuracy the villainy and craftiness of such characters as Bumble, Bill Sikes, Pecksniff, Uriah Heep and Squeers. Undoubtedly from his earliest childhood he had possessed the quick perception, the instinct, which could read in people's characters their tendencies toward good and evil, and throughout his life he valued this ability above literary skill and finish. Mr. [John] Forster makes a point of this in his biography, speaking of the noticeable traits in him: "What I had most, indeed, to notice in him at the very outset of his career, was his indifference to any praise of his performances on their merely literary merit, compared with the higher recognition of them as bits of actual life, with the meaning and purpose on their part, and the responsibility on his, of realities rather than creatures of fancy."

But he was always pleased with praise, and always modest and grateful in returning it. "How can I thank you?" he writes to a friend who was expressing his pleasure at *Oliver Twist*. "Can I do better than by saying that the sense of poor Oliver's reality, which I know you have had from the first, has been the highest of all praise to me? None that has been lavished upon me have I felt half so much as that appreciation of my intent and meaning. Your notices make me very grateful, but very proud, so have a care."

The impressions which were later converted into motives and plots for his stories he imbibed often in his earliest childhood. The crusade against the Yorkshire schools which is waged in *Nicholas Nickleby*, is the working out of some of these childish impressions. He writes himself of them: "I cannot call to mind how I came to hear about Yorkshire schools, when I was not a very robust child, sitting in by-places near Rochester Castle with a head full of [characters] Partridge, Strap, Tom Pipes and Sancho Panza, but I know my first impressions of the schools were picked up at this time." We can imagine how deeply the wrongs must have sunk into the sensitive heart of the child, rankling there through many years, to bear fruit in the scourging of them and their abuses from the land. While he was at work upon *Nicholas Nickleby*, he sent one of his characteristic letters in reply to a little boy—Master Hasting Hughes—who wrote to ask him to make some changes in the story. As some of you may not have read this letter, and as it is so extremely amusing, I shall quote part of it:

DOUGHTY STREET, LONDON.

December 12th, 1838.

Respected Sir: I have given Squeers one cut on the neck, and two on the head, at which he appeared much surprised, and began to cry, which, being a cowardly thing, is just what I should have expected from him—wouldn't you?

I have carefully done what you told me in your letter about the lamb and the two 'sheeps' for the little boys. They have also had some good ale and porter and some wine. I am sorry you did not say what wine you would like them to have. I gave them some sherry, which they liked very much, except one boy who was a little sick and choked a good deal. He was rather greedy, and that's the truth, and I believe it went the wrong way, which I say served him, right, and I hope you will say so too. Nick has had his roast lamb, as you said he was to, but he could not eat it all, and says if you do not mind his doing so he should like to have the rest hashed to-morrow with some greens, which he is very fond of, and so am I. He said he did not like to have his porter hot, for he thought it spoilt the flavour, so I let him have it cold. You should have seen him drink it. I thought he never would have left off. I also gave him three pounds in money, all in sixpences to make it seem more, and he said directly that he should give more than half to his mamma and sister, and divide the rest with poor Smike. And I say he is a good fellow for saying so; and if anybody says he isn't, I am ready to fight him whenever they like—there!

Fanny Squeers shall be attended to, depend upon it. Your drawing of her is very like, except that I do not think the hair is quite curly enough. The nose is particularly like hers, and so are the legs. She is a nasty, disagreeable thing, and I know it will make her very cross when she sees it, and what I say is that I hope it may. You will say the same, I know—at least I think you will.

Dickens's Literary Output Varied

The amount of work which he could accomplish varied greatly at certain times, though in its entirety it was so immense. When he became the man of letters, and ceased the irregular, unmethodical life of the reporter, his mornings were invariably spent at his desk. The time between breakfast and luncheon, with an occasional extension of a couple of hours into the afternoon, were given over to his creations. The exceptions were when he was taking a holiday or resting, though even when ostensibly employed in the latter, cessation from story writing meant the answering of letters and the closer attention to his business matters, so that but little of real rest ever came into his later life.

While in Italy he gave a fragmentary diary of his daily life in a letter to a friend, and the routine was there very much what it was at home. "I am in a regular ferocious excitement with the Chimes; get up at seven; have a cold bath before breakfast; and blaze away, wrathful and red-hot, until three o'clock or so, when I usually knock off (unless it rains) for the day. I am fierce to finish in a spirit bearing some affinity to that of truth and mercy, and to shame the cruel and the wicked, but it is hard work." His entire discomfort under sound interruptions is also shown in the above, in his reference to *The Chimes*, and the effect which they had upon him.

Despite his regularity of working hours, as I have said, the amount of work which my father accomplished varied greatly. His manuscripts were usually written upon white "slips," though sometimes upon blue paper, and there were many mornings when it would be impossible for him to fill one of these. He writes on one occasion: "I am sitting at home, patiently waiting for Oliver Twist, who has not yet arrived." And, indeed, "Oliver" gave him considerable trouble, in the course of his adventures, by his disinclination to be put upon paper easily. This slowness in writing marked more prominently the earlier period of my father's literary career, though these "blank days," when his brain refused to work, were of occasional occurrence to the end. He was very critical of his own labors, and would bring nothing but the best of his brain to the art which he so dearly loved—his venerated mistress. But, on the other hand, the amount of work which he would accomplish at other times was almost incredible. During a long sojourn at Lausanne [in Switzerland] he writes: "I have not been idle since I have been here. I had a good deal to write for Lord John about the ragged schools; so I set to work and did that. A good deal to Miss Coutts, in reference to her charitable projects; so I set to work and did that. Half of the children's New Testament to write, or pretty nearly. I set to work and did that. Next, I cleared off the greater part of such correspondence as I had rashly pledged myself to, and then— began Dombey!"

I know of only one occasion on which he employed an amanuensis, and my aunt is my authority for the following, concerning this one time: "The book which your father dictated to me was *A Child's History of England*. The reason for my being used in this capacity of secretary was that *Bleak House* was being written at the same time, and your father would dictate to me while walking about the room, as a relief after his long, sedentary imprisonment. The history was being written for *Household Words*, and *Bleak House* also as a serial, so he had both weekly and monthly work on hand at the same time." The history was dedicated: "To my own dear children, whom I hope it will help, by-and-by, to read with interest larger and better books upon the same subject."

Dickens's Early Life Made Him Sympathetic to the Poor

Gareth Jenkins

Gareth Jenkins is a writer for Socialist Review.

Charles Dickens's radicalism was formed by the poverty his family was thrust into when he was a young boy, Jenkins suggests in the following viewpoint. Throughout his career, Dickens trumpeted individual initiative, the critic states. While the early Dickens novels show the individual prevailing against adversity, Jenkins finds the later works to be more pessimistic, showing the inhumanity of society.

W hat would Dickens have made of Britain as it celebrates his bicentenary? For all the differences, he would have been only too familiar with the shameless piling up of wealth, the poor struggling to survive, the penny-pinching of welfare, and the lofty contempt of our rulers.

The Insecurity of His Early Life

In his day Dickens was known for his reforming zeal—one of his novels was accused of "sullen socialism". He was none too keen on the aristocratic coterie that ran Britain. He had faith, as he put it, in the people governed rather than the people governing. He loathed society's treatment of children and particularly the way in which education turned young minds into little fact-filled pitchers.

If he was more than the jolly inventor of the Christmas spirit, what kind of radical was Dickens?

Dickens's formative years were the late 1830s and early 1840s—a period of turbulent capitalist transformation of the great cities, of enormous social conflict between different social forces, and of fierce ideological turmoil. Dickens's own family knew something of this everlasting uncertainty. They moved house frequently to stay one step ahead of their creditors. Dickens's father was imprisoned for debt and Dickens himself was removed from school to do menial work in a shoe-blacking factory.

These were humiliating experiences, about which Dickens kept quiet. At the same time he was acutely aware, through direct experience, of the wretched lives of the poor. The horror Dickens felt at the poverty into which he so nearly descended and his sympathy for its victims form the imaginative axis of much of his writing. They also define his radicalism.

Social dislocation also opened up—in this new bourgeois world—the possibility of using your own talents to get ahead in life. Dickens was a case in point: As something of a one-man literary factory, he succeeded by constantly producing a stream of novels, short stories and journalism that appealed to a new public. He had nothing but contempt for the kind of aristocratic assumption that birth and breeding were owed a living. In this sense Dickens was an impatient radical, eager to rid society of the indolent parasitism that strangled individual initiative.

At the same time, he was deeply suspicious of another strand of radicalism shared by many of those who, like him, wanted to reform the existing order. This was a radicalism that focused on disciplining the poor and the vulnerable. "Reforming" the poor law and the workhouse to make "welfare" (such as it was) as unpleasant as possible for the "work-shy" provoked Dickens's wrath—as seen in *Oliver Twist* (1839). This was the period when "free market" ideas, alongside the capitalist interests they served, were making inroads. The idea that those at the bottom of society had only themselves to blame if they starved struck Dickens as callous when there was wealth enough to satisfy their needs.

An illustration from Charles Dickens's Great Expectations *shows Joe Gargery provoked to violence in his smithy. In the background his brother-in-law Pip, the hero of the novel, works the bellows.* © World History Archive/Alamy.

Dickens Addressed Social Issues

Dickens appealed to the idea that we share a common humanity beyond social division. He did so in order to fight what was fast becoming the reality of bourgeois society: its lack of common interests. Appealing to the "good" side of bourgeois society against its "bad" side is something we see in Dickens's *A Christmas Carol* (1843) and the way in which the heartless, tight-fisted Scrooge becomes a generous benefactor of the poor. Sentimental, yes, but it was a protest against the notion that there was no alternative.

The early Dickens novels are open and episodic. The serial technique of novel writing in monthly, and occasionally weekly, parts (a technique which Dickens virtually invented) meant that he could reach a new audience. It gave him the freedom to introduce new characters and address issues (the reality of the poor law or cruelty in education that might challenge this audience's feelings and conscience). The breadth of form also enabled him to vastly expand the social world of the novel: The rich and wealthy have to make way for characters from the lower classes. Plebeian voices jostle for the right to be heard.

The "opening up" of society—seen, for example, in the dislocation caused by the building of railways in the heart of London described so memorably in *Dombey and Son* (1848)—brings these excluded voices into proximity with establishment voices. Thus the haughty businessman, Mr Dombey, is forced to hear condolences from the train driver, whose wife has nursed his dying son—something that offends his sense of social distance.

These plebeian characters often lack rounded personalities or individuality. Circumstances have reduced them to little more than a defining and fixed phrase or gesture. But the way in which they constantly invent themselves through their idiomatic use of language bestows life and energy on them. If human beings are disempowered, the city that surrounds them can seem to take on a life of its own, as if animated by forces that humanity cannot control. You cannot read much Dickens without being struck by the way his novels capture, in comic and grotesque form, central aspects of capitalist alienation.

Dickens Became More Pessimistic

The later Dickens is less convinced that the individual can prevail against an increasingly constraining society. The tone is less exuberant, the comedy darker. His novels from the 1850s and 1860s are tighter in form, less episodic, as if in recognition that systems—legal, judicial and financial systems—bind the individual and every gesture of benevolence to impotence, or worse. In *Bleak House* (1853) individuals cannot escape the grip of a self-consuming lawsuit over an inheritance. In *Little Dorrit* (1857) physical, mental and linguistic imprisonment traps people in deadening notions of what is genteel and proper. Dickens's last complete novel, *Our Mutual Friend* (1865), shows society as a dust heap, charity as a business and orphans in danger of being farmed out as marketable commodities (quite a shift from the early Dickens).

Dickens runs into difficulty when, instead of speaking for the excluded, he is confronted with the excluded speaking for themselves. Urging social reform on behalf of the victims, or championing their rights, is one thing—the focus is on the moral and spiritual qualities of the hero, who can move among the deprived but is not one of them. It's quite another when the victims themselves constitute an active subject and need no hero to represent them. Dickens's weakest novels are those in which the victims represent themselves as a rioting or revolutionary mob—*Barnaby Rudge* (1841) and *A Tale of Two Cities* (1859)—or with the potential to become a collective trade union force (as in his 1854 "condition of England" novel, *Hard Times*).

Dickens Explores True Gentility

Dickens's weakness is particularly obvious in his proneness to sentimentalise and idealise women. Women are reduced to types: the child bride, the saintly figure, the object of romantic desire, or the "fallen woman". They operate in the context of the domestic ideal that the hero yearns for—as, for example, in *David Copperfield* (1850), where David's intellectually challenged child bride conveniently dies to make way for the "perfect" wife that complements his attainment as a writer.

Occasionally there are women characters that suggest Dickens was dimly aware of the real complexity in women's lives. This is the case in his late novels—particularly *Great Expectations* (1861), in which Dickens came closest to tackling the problematic nature of the bourgeois hero. Both *Great Expectations* and *David Copperfield* centre on the question of how to become a true "gentleman"—not because of birth but because of attainment.

David's youthful protector and mentor, [James] Steerforth, may have aristocratic grace and charm but he behaves in a selfish and destructive way, particularly towards women. The true gentility David learns depends on bourgeois qualities of self-reliance and dedication to the domestic ideal.

But there is a nasty side to bourgeois advancement, represented by the "umble" Uriah Heep, who uses cunning, deceit and hypocrisy to advance in the world. Uriah's and David's social status may not be so different but the disgust, verging on the physical, David feels for Uriah (quite unlike the regret David feels for the aristocratic Steerforth's fate) points to something else. The contrast in emotional response suggests that we are meant to believe that David's true nature, beneath the accidents of early deprivation or poverty, is genteel: He could never behave like Uriah.

In *Great Expectations*, arguably Dickens's greatest novel, gentility is explored more critically through a searching exploration of shame and the consequences of a person denying their origins.

The orphan Pip, unlike the orphaned David, is of genuinely humble origins: the family breadwinner, Joe Gargery, works as a blacksmith. What propels him towards becoming a gentleman isn't the bourgeois ideal of hard work and enlightened morality but deep shame about his social status as well as the baseless (but telling) assumption that the hidden source of his inheritance is socially superior.

Eventually Pip learns the real source of his wealth: not the decayed aristocratic Miss Havisham, but the convict [Abel] Magwitch, whom Pip had helped as a child. When Magwitch secretly returns from the penal colony of Australia to see the gentleman he has made, Pip is shattered by the realisation that he has turned into a kind of Frankenstein's monster (Dickens refers to the story)—a monster of ingratitude. By repudiating his past (most clearly seen in the episode when Pip is visited by Joe in London and is deeply ashamed of having to acknowledge the relationship), he has sacrificed his humanity.

There is no way back. For once Dickens holds back from providing a sentimental ending. Pip may be repentant but there is no reward. Estella, the woman he loves and whose contempt for such a common, labouring lad spurred his youthful desire for advancement, has become as dehumanised by gentility as he has. Dickens leaves it unclear as to whether they marry—his first ending leaves them separated; the second, published ending is ambivalent.

This is a novel with no confidence that anything humane can be salvaged from bourgeois society—a sentiment worth remembering amidst the celebrations that will surround his bicentenary.

A *Tale of Two Cities* and Class Conflict

Dickens's Ambiguity Regarding the Revolution Leaves the Story Without a Moral Conclusion

John Gross

John Gross was one of the most important British literary critics of the twentieth century. During his career, he served as editor of the Times Literary Supplement, *book critic for the* New York Times, *and literary editor of the* New Statesman *and* Spectator *magazines. He was the author of numerous books, including* The Rise and Fall of the Man of Letters.

A Tale of Two Cities displays Charles Dickens's ambivalence about the French Revolution, according to Gross in the following viewpoint. Dickens is equally critical of the excessive brutality of the revolutionaries and of the aristocratic society whose oppressive cruelty spawned the Revolution, Gross suggests. In this contradictory context, Gross asserts, Dickens achieves no real conclusion—for the characters or for the moral questions raised.

A *Tale of Two Cities* is a tale of two heroes. The theme of the double has such obvious attractions for a writer preoccupied with disguises, rival impulses, and hidden affinities that it is surprising that Dickens didn't make more use of it elsewhere. But no one could claim that his handling of the device is very successful here, or that he has managed to range the significant forces of the novel behind [Sydney] Carton and [Charles] Darnay. Darnay is, so to speak, the accredited representative of Dickens in the novel, the 'normal' hero for whom a happy ending is still possible. It has been noted, interestingly

John Gross, "A Tale of Two Cities," *Dickens and the Twentieth Century*, ed. by John Gross and Gabriel Pearson. Copyright © 1962 Routledge and Kegan. Reproduced by permission of Taylor & Francis Books UK.

enough, that he shares his creator's initials—and that is pretty well the only interesting thing about him. Otherwise he is a pasteboard character, completely undeveloped. His position as an exile, his struggles as a language teacher, his admiration for George Washington are so many openings thrown away.

Carton's Sacrifice Was Meaningless

Carton, of course, is a far more striking figure. He belongs to the line of cultivated wastrels who play an increasingly large part in Dickens's novels during the second half of his career, culminating in Eugene Wrayburn [character in *Our Mutual Friend*]; his clearest predecessor, as his name indicates, is the luckless Richard Carstone of *Bleak House*. He has squandered his gifts and drunk away his early promise; his will is broken, but his intellect is unimpaired. In a sense, his opposite is not Darnay at all, but the aggressive Stryver, who makes a fortune by picking his brains. Yet there is something hollow about his complete resignation to failure: his self-abasement in front of Lucie [Manette], for instance. ('I am like one who died young. . . . I know very well that you can have no tenderness for me. . . .') For, stagy a figure though he is, Carton does suggest what Thomas Hardy calls 'fearful unfulfilments'; he still has vitality, and it is hard to believe that he has gone down without a struggle. The total effect is one of energy held unnaturally in check: the bottled-up frustration which Carton represents must spill over somewhere.

Carton's and Darnay's fates are entwined from their first meeting, at the Old Bailey trial. Over the dock there hangs a mirror: 'crowds of the wicked and the wretched had been reflected in it, and had passed from its surface and this earth's together. Haunted in a most ghastly manner that abominable place would have been, if the glass could ever have rendered back its reflections, as the ocean is one day to give up its dead.' After Darnay's acquittal we leave him with Carton, 'so like each other in feature, so unlike in manner, both reflected in the glass above them'. Reflections, like ghosts, suggest unreality and self-division, and at the end of the same day Carton stares at his own image in the glass and upbraids it: 'Why should you particularly like a man who resembles you? There is nothing in you to like: you know that. Ah, confound you! . . . Come on, and have it out in plain words! You hate the fellow.' In front of the mirror, Carton thinks of changing places with Darnay; at the end of the book, he is to take the other's death upon him. Dickens prepares the ground: when Darnay is in jail, it is Carton who strikes Mr. Lorry as having 'the wasted air of a prisoner', and when he is visited by Carton on the rescue attempt, he thinks at first that he is 'an apparition of his own imagining'. But Dickens is determined to stick by Darnay: a happy ending *must* be possible. As Lorry and his party gallop to safety with the drugged Darnay, there is an abrupt switch to the first person: 'The wind is rushing after us, and the clouds are flying after us, and the moon is plunging after us, and the whole wild night is in pursuit of us; but so far, we are pursued by nothing else.' *We* can make our escape, however narrowly; Carton, expelled from our system, must be abandoned to his fate.

But the last word is with Carton—the most famous last word in Dickens, in fact. Those who take a simplified view of Dickens's radicalism, or regard him as one of nature's Marxists, can hardly help regretting that *A Tale of Two Cities* should end as it does. They are bound to feel, with Edgar Johnson, that 'instead of merging, the truth of revolution and the truth of sacrifice are made to appear in conflict'. A highly personal, indeed a unique crisis cuts across public issues and muffles the political message. But this is both to sentimentalize Dickens's view of the Revolution, and to miss the point about Carton. The cynical judgment that his sacrifice was trifling, since he had nothing to live for, is somewhat nearer the mark. Drained of the will to live, he is shown in the closing chapters of the book as a man courting death, and embracing it when it comes. . . .

Sydney Carton, being played by British actor Ronald Colman, is being led to the guillotine by two soldiers in a scene from the 1935 movie adaptation of A Tale of Two Cities. © Hulton Archive/Moviepix/Getty Images.

Dickens Shows the Horror of Mob Violence

By this time the Revolution has become simply the agency of death, the storm that overwhelms the city. Or rather, all the pent-up fury and resentment that is allowed no outlet in the 'personal' side of the book, with Carton kowtowing to Stryver and nobly renouncing Lucie, boils over in revolutionary violence: Dickens dances the Carmagnole [a song and dance popular during the French Revolution], and howls for blood with the mob. Frightened by the forces which he has released, he views the Revolution with hatred and disgust; he doesn't record a single incident in which it might be shown as beneficent, constructive or even tragic. Instead, it is described time and again in terms of pestilence and madness. Dickens will hear nothing of noble aspirations; the disorder of the whole period is embodied in the dervishes who dance the Carmagnole—'no fight could have been half so terrible'. Confronted with the crowd, Dickens reaches for his gun; he looks into eyes 'which any unbrutalized beholder would have given twenty years of life, to have petrified with a well-directed gun'. That 'well-directed' has the true ring of outraged rate-paying respectability, while the image seems oddly out of place in a book which has laid so much stress on the stony faces and petrified hearts of the aristocracy.

Dickens can only deal with mob violence in a deliberately picturesque story set in the past. But *A Tale of Two Cities*, written by a middle-aged man who could afford a longer perspective at a time when Chartism was already receding into history, is not quite analogous to *Barnaby Rudge*. There, however contemptible, we are meant to find the world of Sir John Chester, the riots are an explosion of madness and nothing more. But the French Revolution compels Dickens to acquire a theory of history, however primitive: 'crush humanity out of shape once more, under similar hammers, and it will twist itself into the same tortured forms'. The revolutionaries return evil for evil; the guillotine is the product not of innate depravity but of intolerable oppression. If Dickens's sympathies shift towards the aristocrats as soon as they become victims, he can also show a grim restraint; he underlines the horror of Foulon's death [referring to the death of French politician

Foulon de Doué], strung up with a bunch of grass tied to his back (how his imagination pounces on such a detail!), but he never allows us to forget who Foulon was. Nor does he have any sympathy with those who talk of the Revolution 'as though it were the only harvest under the skies that had never been sown', although he himself is at times plainly tempted to treat it as an inexplicable calamity, a rising of the sea (the gaoler [jailer] at La Force has the bloated body of a drowned man, and so forth) or a rising of fire: the flames which destroy the château of St. Evrémonde 'blow from the infernal regions', convulsing nature until the lead boils over inside the stone fountains. But cause and effect are never kept out of sight for long; Dickens is always reminding himself that the Revolution, though 'a frightful moral disorder', was born of 'unspeakable suffering, intolerable oppression, and heartless indifference'. Society was diseased before the fever broke out: the shattered cask of wine which at the outset falls on the 'crippling' stones of Saint Antoine is scooped up in little mugs of 'mutilated' earthenware.

But to grasp a patient's medical history is not to condone his disease, and Dickens is unyielding in his hostility to the crowd. The buzzing of the flies on the scent for carrion at the Old Bailey trial and the mass-rejoicing at Roger Cly's funeral are early indications of what he feels. The courtroom in Paris is also full of buzzing and stirring, but by this time the atmosphere has become positively cannibalistic; a jury of dogs has been empanelled to try the deer, Madame Defarge 'feasts' on the prisoner, Jacques III, with his very Carlylean [after historian of the French Revolution, Thomas Carlyle] croak, is described as an epicure.

Whatever Dickens's motives, a good deal of this is no doubt perfectly valid; morbid fantasies can still prompt shrewd observations, as when we are shown Darnay, the prisoner of half an hour, already learning to count the steps as he is led away to his cell. In particular, Dickens recognizes the ways in which a period of upheaval can obliterate the individual personality; there is no more telling detail in the book than the roll call of the condemned containing the names of a prisoner who has died in jail and two who have already been guillotined, all of them forgotten. Insane suspicion, senseless massacres, the rise to power of the worst elements: in the era of Gladstonian [referring to British politician William Gladstone] budgets Dickens understands the workings of a police state.

But it would be ludicrous to claim very much for the accuracy of Dickens's account of the French Revolution as such. There are scarcely any references to the actual course of events, and no suggestion at all that the Revolution had an intellectual or idealistic content, while the portrayal of fanaticism seems childish if we compare it even with something as one-sided as *The Gods Are Athirst* [novel by Anatole France]. For the purposes of the novel, the Revolution is the Defarges, and although Carton foresees that Defarge in his turn will perish on the guillotine, he has no inkling of how the whole internecine [conflict within a group that is injurious to all sides] process will ever come to a halt. As for Madame Defarge, she is as much driven by fate as the stony-hearted Marquis, with his coachmen cracking their whips like the Furies: the time has laid 'a dreadfully disfiguring hand upon her'. Her last entry is her most dramatic. Miss Pross is bathing her eyes to rid herself of feverish apprehensions, when she suddenly appears—materializes, one might say—in the doorway:

> The basin fell to the ground broken, and the water flowed to the feet of Madame Defarge. By strange stern ways, and through much staining blood, those feet had come to meet that water.

We are reminded, by rather too forcible a contrast, of the broken cask of red wine which prefaces Madame Defarge's first appearance in the novel. Her element, from the very start, is blood.

Dickens's Genius Shows Through

Still, *A Tale of Two Cities* is not a private nightmare, but a work which continues to give pleasure. Dickens's drives and conflicts are his raw material, not the source of his artistic power, and in itself the fact that the novel twists the French Revolution into a highly personal fantasy proves nothing: so, after all, does *The Scarlet Pimpernel* [by Baroness Emmuska Orczy]. Everything depends on the quality of the writing—which is usually one's cue, in talking about Dickens, to pay tribute to his exuberance and fertility. Dickens's genius inheres in minute particulars; later we may discern patterns of symbolism and imagery, a design which lies deeper than the plot, but first we are struck by the lavish heaping up of acute observations, startling similes, descriptive flourishes, circumstantial embroidery. Or such is the case with every Dickens novel except for the *Tale*, which is written in a style so grey and unadorned that many readers are reluctant to grant it a place in the canon at all. Dickens wouldn't be Dickens if there weren't occasional touches like the 'hospital procession of negro cupids, several headless and all cripples', which Mr. Lorry notices framing the mirror in his hotel (or the whitewashed cupid 'in the coolest linen' on the ceiling of his Paris office, which makes its appearance three hundred pages later). But for the most part one goes to the book for qualities which are easier to praise than to illustrate or examine: a rapid tempo which never lets up from the opening sentence, and a sombre eloquence which saves Carton from mere melodrama, and stamps an episode like the running down of the child by the Marquis's carriage on one's mind with a primitive intensity rarely found after Dickens's early novels, like an outrage committed in a fairy tale.

A Tale of Two Cities Lacks Humor

But it must be admitted that the *Tale* is in many ways a thin and uncharacteristic work, bringing the mounting despair of the eighteen-fifties to a dead end rather than ushering in the triumphs of the 'sixties. In no other novel, not even *Hard Times*, has Dickens's natural profusion been so drastically pruned. Above all, the book is notoriously deficient in humour. One falls—or flops—back hopefully on the Crunchers, but to small avail. True, the comic element parodies the serious action: Jerry, like his master, is a 'Resurrection-Man', but on the only occasion that we see him rifling a grave it turns out to be empty, while his son's panic-stricken flight with an imaginary coffin in full pursuit is nightmarish rather than funny. As comic characters the Crunchers are forced and mechanical; such true humour as there is in the book is rather to be found in scattered observations, but settings and characters are colourful rather than grotesque. Obviously Dickens's humour is many things, but it is usually bound up with a sense of almost magical power over nature: to distort, exaggerate, yoke together or dissolve is to manipulate and control external reality. In Dickens people are always taking on the qualities of objects with which they come into contact, and *vice versa*: a basic Dickensian trick of style, which makes its appearance as early as the opening pages of *Sketches by Boz*, where there is a fine passage ('Our Parish', Chapter VII) on the 'resemblance and sympathy' between a man's face and the knocker on his front door. Such transformations are not unknown in *A Tale of Two Cities*—there is the obstinate door at Tellson's [Bank] with the weak rattle in its throat, for example—but they occur less frequently than in any other Dickens novel, and there is a corresponding lack of power for which a neatly constructed plot is small compensation.

Contrary to what might be expected, this absence of burlesque is accompanied by a failure to present society in any depth. *A Tale of Two Cities* may deal with great political events, but nowhere else in the later work of Dickens is there less sense of society as a living organism. Evrémondes and Defarges alike seem animated by sheer hatred; we hear very little of the stock social themes, money, hypocrisy, and snobbery. Tellson's, musty and cramped and antiquated, makes an excellent Dickensian set piece, but it is scarcely followed up. Jarvis Lorry, too, is a sympathetic version of the fairy godfather, a saddened Cheeryble who repines at spending his days 'turning a vast pecuniary mangle', but this side of his character is only lightly sketched in. He may glance through the iron bars of his office window 'as if they were ruled for figures too, and everything under the clouds were a sum', but he is more important as a protective, reassuring figure: in times of revolution Tellson's mustiness becomes a positive virtue.

Dickens Is a Moralist

The lack of social density shows up Dickens's melodrama to disadvantage. This is partly a question of length, since in a short novel everything has to be worked in as best it can: Barsad will inevitably turn out to be Miss Pross's long-lost brother, Defarge has to double as Doctor [Alexandre] Manette's old servant, and so forth. But there is a deeper reason for feeling more dissatisfaction with the artificial plot here than one does with equally far-fetched situations elsewhere in Dickens. Where society is felt as an all-enveloping force, Dickens is able to turn the melodramatic conventions which he inherited to good use; however preposterous the individual coincidences, they serve an important symbolic function. The world is more of a piece than we suppose, Dickens is saying, and our fates are bound up, however cut off from one another we may appear: the pestilence from Tom-all-Alone's [in *Bleak House*] really will spread to the Dedlock mansion, and sooner or later the river in which Gaffer Hexam [a character in *Our Mutual Friend*] fishes for corpses will flow through the Veneering drawing room. In a word, we can't have Miss Havisham without [Abel] Magwitch [characters in *Great Expectations*]. But without a thick social atmosphere swirling round them, the characters of *A Tale of Two Cities* stand out in stark melodramatic isolation; the spotlight is trained too sharply on the implausibilities of the plot, and the stage is set for Sir John Martin-Harvey [a British actor] and *The Only Way* [stage adaptation of *A Tale of Two Cities*]. So, too, the relentless workings of destiny are stressed rather clumsily by such a bare presentation; Madame Defarge points the finger of fate a little too vigorously, and there is a tendency towards heavy repetitions and parallelisms, brought out by the chapter headings, 'A Hand at Cards' and 'The Game Made', 'Dusk' and 'Darkness', and so forth.

Yet despite the dark mood in which it was conceived, the *Tale* isn't a wholly gloomy work; nor is the final impression which it leaves with us one of a wallow of self-pity on the scaffold. We are told of Darnay in the condemned cell (or is it Carton?) that

> his hold on life was strong, and it was very, very hard to loosen; by gradual efforts and degrees unclosed a little here, it clenched the tighter there; and when he brought his strength to bear on that hand and it yielded this was closed again. There was a hurry, too, in all his thoughts, a turbulent and heated working of his heart, that contended against resignation.

And near the end, as Miss Pross grapples with Madame Defarge, Dickens speaks of 'the vigorous tenacity of love, always so much stronger than hate'. The gruesome events of the book scarcely bear out such a judgment, yet as an article of faith, if not as a statement of the literal truth, it is curiously impressive. For all the sense of horror which he must have felt stirring within him when he wrote *A Tale of Two Cities*, Dickens remained a moralist and a preacher, and it was his saving strength. But if the author doesn't succumb with Carton, neither does he escape with Darnay. At the end of the book 'we' gallop away not to safety and Lucie, but to the false hopes of Pip, the thwarted passion of Bradley Headstone, the divided life of John Jasper [characters in *Great Expectations, Our Mu-*

tual Friend, and *The Mystery of Edwin Drood*, respectively]. Nothing is concluded, and by turning his malaise into a work of art, Dickens obtains parole, not release: the prison will soon be summoning him once more.

Dickens Shows His Support for the Working Class in *A Tale of Two Cities*

T.A. Jackson

An author, journalist, and lecturer, T.A. Jackson was a founder of both the Communist Party and the Socialist Party of Great Britain.

Charles Dickens was wholeheartedly on the side of the working class and opposed to the aristocracy in A Tale of Two Cities, *argues Jackson in the following viewpoint. The French Revolution was a triumph for the common man and the only way of achieving justice in France, Jackson maintains. Jackson further argues that Dickens surpasses the boldness of many other authors by warning the undeserving privileged class of an "Avenging Fate."*

[A Tale of Two Cities] has as its background the great French Revolution. . . . [It] demonstrates unmistakably—and one might add, aggressively—Dickens' sympathy with the people in revolt, with their revolt itself, and with, too, within limits, even their infuriated infliction of vengeance upon their oppressors. This was a far bolder, and a far more significant thing to do, in 1859, than might seem possible today [1937].

Revolution Was Necessary to Achieve Justice

It is true that the same year saw the production both of [Karl] Marx's *[A Contribution to the] Critique of Political Economy*, and of [Charles] Darwin's *The Origin of Species*. But the coming of these far-reachingly revolutionary works only the more emphasized the conservatism, and the anti-revolutionary bias of the mental world into which they were born. That Marx should have retired into relative seclusion to perfect his economic studies was in itself evidence that, at that time, "only a literary battle was possible." That Darwin's work should have been needed, seventy years after the work of [French biologist Jean-Baptiste] Lamarck, proves the same thing; as does the fact that the *Origin* gained its first widespread popularity because it was thought to provide theoretical weapons against any sort of popular revolutionary uprising. . . .

What a reception [John] Ruskin met the year following the appearance of all these three works—the *Critique*, the *Origin*, and *A Tale of Two Cities*. [Editor's note: John Ruskin's essays, *Unto This Last*, received a hostile reception from a conservative audience]. It might, indeed, be argued, that only Dickens' well-established popularity saved him from a denunciation similar to that which befell Ruskin. The supercilious shrugged their shoulders, and put it down to Dickens' ingrained "lowness"—to the fact that he "couldn't understand a *gentleman*"—and noted it as further evidence of the decline of Dickens' genius since *Bleak House*, since *Martin Chuzzlewit*, or (by the most supercilious) since *[The] Pickwick [Papers]*. Anyway, since its revolutionary implications were bound up with—and somewhat obscured by—an intensely dramatic story culminating in a finely melodramatic scene of heroic self-sacrifice, *A Tale of Two Cities* could be and was allowed to pass as a moral story in which the horrors of the French Revolution were provided with a suitable corrective in the noble resignation and self-denial of Sydney Carton.

And that view, for bourgeois criticism in general, has remained the dominant view; all the more so as it has been crystallized by the dramatization of the novel under the title of *The Only Way*—in which a first-class actor made a reputation in the role of Sydney Carton.

Nonetheless it is a false view. It is with *A Tale of Two Cities* as it is with *Little Dorrit,* and indeed with all the novels of Dickens' third period—the *real* drama is an implicit drama, which the foreground action-drama serves only to symbolize.

Parallels in Societal Commentary

The ground theme is indicated in the title of its first part (which Dickens originally intended to make the title of the novel itself): "Recalled to Life." A prisoner imprisoned for more than twenty years, is "recalled to life," only to find that, by the cruel irony of fate, the very wrong done to him is now used as a means of inflicting further suffering upon him. This, which is the fate of Dr. [Alexandre] Manette in *A Tale of Two Cities,* is, it will be perceived, also the fate of the elder Dorrit and his daughter Amy [in *Little Dorrit*]. In *A Tale of Two Cities* the irony is made more obvious and more poignant since Dr. Manette is imprisoned, not in association in a Marshalsea [prison in England], but in strict solitude in the Bastille [a prison in France]. In each case, release comes "out of the blue." Edward Dorrit is released by a legacy unearthed and made operative primarily by the energetic (if grubby) Mr. Panks. Dr. Manette is released partly by the fall from court favour of the nobleman who had secured his imprisonment and partly by the tidy (but industrious) Jarvis Lorry, manager of Tellson's Bank. Edward Dorrit is forever tormented by the fear that the wrong done to him—his twenty-five years' imprisonment in the Marshalsea—will become known to his disparagement in the Good Society to which his newfound wealth gives him access. This very anxiety is the proximate cause of the loss of his fortune in the Merdle swindle, which, however, proves a blessing in disguise; since it releases Little Dorrit from the wealth which separates her from her Arthur. Dr. Manette's agony is in one sense more subtle—arising as it does from the fact that his adored daughter loves and marries the son and nephew of the aristocratic brothers who had secured his imprisonment. Edward Dorrit is released from his torment by his collapse and death; his daughter Amy is released by the collapse of the Merdle enterprises which follows the suicide of the swindler Merdle. Dr. Manette and his daughter are both released together from their torment by the heroic intervention of Sydney Carton into the revolutionary turmoil which had placed Lucie's husband in peril of his life. In each case the novel closes on a note similar to that of Edmund Spenser's [from *The Faerie Queene*] lines:

Sleep after toil: port after stormy seas,

Ease after war, death after life, does greatly please.

It is impossible to escape the conclusion that this parallelism has an intentional significance. This may possibly have been only partly present to the author's consciousness; but if we are right in seeing in *Bleak House, Hard Times,* and *Little Dorrit* so many phases of expression of one common purpose—a general attack upon the established order of society—we have in *A Tale of Two Cities* a further phase in which Dickens gets nearer than ever to a positive assertion of revolution as the only road to hope, to justice, to peace and to general happiness. In any case the conventional view, which sees Sydney Carton's sacrifice as the primary thematic objective of the novel, is clearly false criticism since it relegates the French Revolution, and the whole dramatic subplot of Madame Defarge's vengeance to the status of mere irrelevancies. More than that—it obscures the whole point that Sydney Carton, by sacrificing his life, achieved a triumphantly redeeming escape, from a life which had been, till then, a dreary torment of failure and frustration. And that this latter is the true view, proved by the fact that it harmonizes exactly with Dickens' view of the French Revolution itself, which was, on his showing, and despite its bloody extravagances, the terrible paroxysm of death and destruction whereby the people achieved a triumphantly redeeming escape from a permanent condition of hunger, subjection, failure and frustration.

Dickens leaves no doubt that this is his meaning. . . .

Dickens Extols the Working Class

It is one of the many charges levelled in disparagement against Dickens' later novels—as compared with his earlier ones—that his plots "grew more mysterious." A generation which has witnessed the rise of the detective novel to the place it occupies today, can hardly see in this "mysteriousness" a blemish. The truth is that Dickens, always a workman, paid the greatest possible attention to the construction of his novels. If in his earlier novels he scattered "characters" with a reckless profusion, in his later works he is at infinite pains to bring on the stage only just so many characters as have actual work to do. His devoted "public" combined with his natural genius made it imperative that he should bring on to his stage a fuller parade of characters than most novelists would care to try to control. And the fact also that his novels all appeared in parts or in installments made it imperative that his every part or installment should contain its specially outstanding incident. Few, if any, writers ever attempted so difficult a task as Dickens did every time he tackled the job of making a large crowd work as a team and weaving a whole hierarchy of main and subsidiary plots and counterplots into a perfectly reticulated whole. And Dickens' skill in this direction was seldom shown to finer advantage than in *A Tale of Two Cities*.

Of its class bias it is superfluous to speak. It ranks as "villains" the whole *ancien régime* [prerevolutionary social and political order in France], aristocracy, absolute monarchy and all their works. It lumps along with aristocracy for equal condemnation all its sycophantic upholders—such as the blatantly self-seeking, philistine, ignoramus, Stryver of the King's Bench Bar. It exalts as heroic, in opposition to all these, the people in all their activities; the oppressed and suffering peasantry; the well-educated and industrious professional men; the faithful and devoted everywhere, down to and including the "failures" such as Sydney Carton. True, the Defarges and their train are shown in a terrible and implacable light. But since every care is taken to show that this implacable lust for vengeance is the direct product of aristocratic pride, selfishness and insolence, it merely adds an extra count to the indictment against the aristocracy that their rule should convert decent and kindly people into avenging furies like the Defarges. True, Jerry Cruncher is a proletarian and is shown as an ugly customer; but even here there is a defence. Quite justly Jerry defends his nefarious "body-snatching" activities by the retort that the well-to-do surgeons, customers at Tellson's Bank, who bribed him heavily to find them "subjects" for dissection, were at least as much to blame as he.

Both Carton and Darnay Make Sacrifices

Most emphatic of all, as an indication of Dickens' standpoint and bias, is his conception of Sydney Carton. That which is usually lost upon readers of *A Tale of Two Cities* and a point which disappears entirely in the dramatized version (for which, of course, Dickens is not responsible), is the fact that the resemblance between Carton and [Charles] Darnay—which makes possible Carton's substitution-sacrifice—does not end at a mere external physical likeness. Both are attracted by, and fall wholly in love with Lucie Manette, and both possess the same reckless generosity and readiness for sacrifice in a worthy cause which in the end leads Carton to take his heroic "only way" out of Lucie's terrible crisis.

Before Carton makes his sacrifice, Darnay has made his. He has sacrificed his title and his inheritance from a sense of their essential injustice and as the only recompense at his command for the wrong these things—titles and feudal rights and privileges—have entailed. Moreover, he has imperilled his personal safety and indeed, his life, to respond to the appeal for protection from a faithful servant, in peril in consequence of doing his duty. Darnay's large-hearted generosity and self-sacrifice precede and create the occasion (as well as the need) for Carton's ultimate self-sacrifice.

Thus by a whole succession of strokes Dickens makes the resemblance between Carton and Darnay extend from their outward appearance to their fundamental character.

There is, of course, an obvious difference. Darnay is as sober and careful as Carton is drunken and careless. In these regards they are opposites. But—and this is usually overlooked—the same contempt of himself which makes Carton a failure and a drunkard is also the quality which makes him prompt to seize the "only way" out of Lucie's difficulties. Thus his supreme virtue has one and the same root as his chief vice.

Dickens here shows, as he often does, his addiction to the doctrine of [Welsh social reformer] Robert Owen: "man's character is made *for* him, and not *by* him." With a little difference in their upbringing and their circumstances, Darnay would have been the failure and the drunkard, and Carton the sober and well-conducted husband. The turn of a hair at a critical stage was enough to separate their respective paths in life, so that their opposition in outward seeming is an expression of the fundamental identity of their characters. Carton is to Darnay and Darnay to Carton only another instance of the great truth: "There, but for the grace of circumstances outside my control, go I!"

That Dickens intends this moral to be drawn is clear from any number of strokes. When Darnay and Carton first meet, Carton behaves insolently—behaves, as he admits to himself, as though he hated Darnay because he shows him, concretely, what he himself might have been. Later on, after Lucie and Darnay are married, their children show a special fondness for Carton. The soundness of an unspoiled child's instincts is one of Dickens' favourite themes.

Nothing is said about Carton's childhood; but from his complete lack of relatives and connections in his manhood it would seem that his parents must have died while he was still an infant. In Darnay's case we know that he was prepared for the sacrifice of his title and his estates by the teaching of his mother—who felt that so cruel had been the injustices worked in their name that there was a curse upon both. It seems a fair inference, and one quite in keeping with Dickens' usual mode of reasoning to suppose that Carton's habitual lack of self-respect or self-regard came from an early training in which he was treated as of no account.

It will be remembered that the theme of a thoroughly good-natured and generous lad, sinking, through lack of proper self-regard, and of any purpose in life, into a drifter, and finally a waster and sot, was one that Dickens had experimented with before. Jingle [in *The Pickwick Papers*] was nearly in this class, but was rescued from it by a native streak of roguery. Dick Swiveller [in *The Old Curiosity Shop*] was clearly a case in point, until he was saved by his discovery of the Marchioness, his illness and the opportune death (and legacy) of his aunt. [James] Steerforth [in *David Copperfield*] is not of this class; he is too much of a fine gentleman, too lacking in real generosity, not fond enough of drink, and altogether too fond of himself to qualify. But, as we noted above, Walter, in *Dombey [and Son]*, was intended to be of this order, until Dickens relented.

Dickens Portrays a Good Man Gone Wrong

With Sydney Carton, therefore, Dickens was able, at last, to work out a theme which he had been wanting for years to work out—the theme of the good man gone wrong through lack or the ballast necessary to compensate for sheer excess of good-nature. It is a theme which, quite clearly, shows the bent of Dickens' mind to have been in the direction of the Helvétius-Owen [referring to Claude Adrien Helvétius, a

French philosopher, and Robert Owen] doctrine of the moral equality of man, and the general perfectibility of human nature. And from this doctrine, as [German social philosophers Karl] Marx and [Friedrich] Engels showed, communism is a logical deduction.

In sum: *A Tale of Two Cities* takes, as clearly as its predecessors had done, the side of the common people against that of the privileged classes. But it adds, more plainly than any of its predecessors, a warning of an Avenging Fate, from fear of which all the privileged, and all those set in authority, would do well to reconsider their ways.

Dickens's Suggestion of the Self as Secondary to the Collective Was a Threat to English Society

Cates Baldridge

Cates Baldridge is an assistant professor of English at Middlebury College.

Critics have found various explanations for Charles Dickens's ambivalent feelings about the French Revolution, Baldridge states in the following viewpoint. Here Baldridge offers his own theory—that Dickens's discomfort with the Victorian insistence on individualism made him more sympathetic to the revolutionaries. Baldridge further suggests that Dickens chose the context of the French Revolution as space to propose a preferable alternative to his society's disease of "impenetrable individuality." In the author's view, Dickens's ambivalence regarding the French Revolution overlays the proposition of a more subtle opening and integration of his contemporary society to something more than "a metropolis in which everyone is virtually 'buried alive.'"

[C]harles] Dickens's ambivalence toward the Revolution he depicts in *A Tale of Two Cities* has been the subject of much thoughtful comment, and over the past few decades a number of differing causes for this ambivalence have been proposed. [Canadian political historian] George Woodcock, for instance, sees in the "vigor" with which the author depicts the scenes of revolutionary violence a kind of vicarious retribution against the society which betrayed him in his youth: "in one self [Dickens] is there, dancing among them, destroy-

Cates Baldridge, "Alternatives to Bourgeois Individualism in A Tale of Two Cities," reprinted with permission from *SEL Studies in English Literarure 1500–1900*, vol. 30, no. 4, Fall 1990, pp. 633–54.

ing prisons and taking revenge for the injustices of childhood." Others have interpreted it as the result of the author's fitful attempts to work out an overarching theory of history, or to adapt [Thomas] Carlyle's ideas on historical necessity to the needs of his fictional genre. Some critics have even pointed out parallels between the methods of the Jacquerie [revolt of peasants against nobles in France] and the literary techniques employed by Dickens himself. What I shall do here is to focus upon one particular aspect of the revolutionary regime in *A Tale* which has received less attention than most, and attempt to put forward a largely political explanation for Dickens's ambivalence concerning it. The aspect I refer to is the Revolution's assertion that the group, the class, the Republic—and not the individual—comprise, or should comprise, the basic unit of society. The corollaries which spring from this belief (and which are themselves fully depicted in the text) will also be considered: that all merely personal claims must defer to those of the polity [governing body] as a whole; that the minds and hearts of citizens must be laid bare to the scrutiny of the community; and that virtues and guilt, rights and responsibilities, inhere in groups rather than in individuals. My contention is that Dickens's deep dissatisfaction with the social relations fostered by his own acquisitive and aggressively individualist society leads him at times to explore with sensitivity and even enthusiasm the liberating possibilities offered by an ideology centered elsewhere than upon the autonomous self. As we shall see, what emerges is a subversive subtext to the narrator's middle-class horror at the collectivist revolutionary ideology promulgated behind the barricades of Paris. . . .

Dickens Had Ambivalent Feelings About the French Revolution

[While] Dickens finds much to disparage in the revolutionary regime he depicts, he nevertheless understands at some level that it offers stark alternatives to the social relations undergirding those aspects of Victorian England that he also thoroughly despises, and that because of this an undercurrent of sympathy makes its way into the text despite his explicit intention to paint the Jacquerie as bloodthirsty, implacable, and deranged. Dickens, who will have no truck with schemes of social amelioration which depend upon class conflict, is far from being a cultural materialist, even when he thunders most vehemently against the abuses of industrial capitalism. One can, however, safely credit him with comprehending a relationship between a society's view of the individual and the economic and interpersonal texture of its daily life. This act of understanding is all I mean to burden Dickens with by way of an "authorial intention," and surely much of the sympathy I find for the Revolution in *A Tale of Two Cities* escaped the novelist's conscious control. . . .

Clearly, we should not expect any such countervailing current of thought as the one outlined above to emerge except in thoroughly disguised and displaced forms, for, as W.J. Harvey long ago pointed out, the assumptions of bourgeois individualism are central to the enterprise of Victorian novelists generally and to that of Dickens in particular. Middle-class orthodoxy posits the discrete human subject as primary and inviolable, a move which Harvey declares to be the indispensable core of classical liberalism, that ideology which he credits both with nurturing the infant genre of the novel in the eighteenth century and assuring its triumph in the nineteenth. Broadly defined, liberalism is, says Harvey, a "state of mind [which] has as its controlling centre an acknowledgment of the plenitude, diversity and individuality of human beings in society, together with the belief that such characteristics are good as ends in themselves," and he goes on to assert that "tolerance, skepticism, [and] respect for the autonomy of others are its watchwords" while "fanaticism and the monolithic creed [are] its abhorrence." Harvey's phrasing may strike some as overly laudatory, but it does help to underscore why the chronically permeable barriers of the self in *A Tale of Two Cities* constitute such a politically dangerous issue: in depicting the Revolution, the text takes pains to portray—and to roundly denounce—a counter-ideology to classical liberalism, in which the claims of the individual are assumed to be secondary to those of the collectivity, and in which the individual is seen as anything but sacrosanct. It should come as little surprise, then, that Dickens's most forceful statement of subversive sympathy for the Revolution's attack upon the idea of the discrete subject, his most anguished confession of ambivalence concerning the bourgeois notion of an inviolable individual, comprises what has long been considered merely an "anomalous" or "digressive" portion of the text—refer specifically to the "Night Shadows" passage, a striking meditation upon the impenetrable barriers separating man from man which has proved perennially troublesome to readers.

> A wonderful fact to reflect upon, that every human creature is constituted to be that profound secret and mystery to every other. A solemn consideration, when I enter a great city by night, that every one of those darkly clustered houses encloses its own secret; that every room in every one of them encloses its own secret; that every beating heart in the hundreds of thousands of breasts there, is, in some of its imaginings, a secret to the heart nearest it! Something of the awfulness, even of Death itself, is referable to this. No more can I turn the leaves of this dear book that I loved, and vainly hope in time to read it all. No more can I look into the depths of this unfathomable water, wherein, as momentary lights glanced into it, I have had glimpses of buried treasure and other things submerged. It was appointed that the book should shut with a spring, for ever and for ever, when I had read but a page. It was appointed that the water should be locked in an eternal frost, when the light was playing on its surface, and I stood in ignorance on the shore. My friend is dead, my neighbour is dead, my love, the darling of my soul, is dead; it is the inexorable consolation

and perpetuation of the secret that was always in that individuality, and which I shall carry in mine to my life's end. In any of the burial-places of this city through which I pass, is there a sleeper more inscrutable than its busy inhabitants are, in their innermost personality, to me, or than I am to them?

The Text of the Novel Suggests Empathy for Community

The relationship of this passage to the major concerns of the novel has struck many a critic as problematic. Some have sought to link it with the rest of the text merely by pointing out its similarities to Carlyle's practice of dramatizing the miraculous hidden within the mundane, and thus to account for it as yet another example of the literary influence of Dickens's occasional mentor. A more ambitious explanation of its thematic significance is attempted by [historicist literary critic] Catherine Gallagher. She, claiming that Dickens depicts the revolutionary ideology as ruthlessly inquisitive in order to make his own, novelistic invasion of the private sphere appear benign by comparison, sees the passage as a reassuring statement that novelists are needed by modern society to overcome a "perpetual scarcity of intimate knowledge," despite the lines' melancholy ring. . . . Most critics, however, follow the lead of Sylvère Monod in simply seeing it as an anomaly. Monod, who posits several distinct narrators for *A Tale* asserts that he who speaks this address is employing "the philosopher's I" and that such a device "is used for general statements, not in order to convey any impression of the narrator as an individual person." J.M. Rignall agrees, insisting that "the brooding, first-person voice is never heard again in the novel," that the passage is at best awkwardly related to the scene which immediately follows it, and that it cannot be said to illuminate "the general condition of life as it appears in the novel."

It is Rignall's contention that I specifically wish to take issue with, for I believe that there is in fact a broadly thematic

Portrait painting of Scottish satirical writer, essayist, historian, and social commentator Thomas Carlyle (1795–1881), who was a friend and mentor of Charles Dickens. Carlyle's book, The French Revolution: A History, *greatly influenced the writing of* A Tale of Two Cities. © Archive Images.

resonance to the passage—a resonance which is crucial to the book's attitudes concerning bourgeois individualism and its supposedly detested alternatives. To begin with, it is significant that all the above critics, whatever their varying degrees of bafflement or insight, call attention to the passage's tone, for it is that aspect of the "digression" which, I believe, can most quickly lead us into its involvement with the novel's political contradictions. While the adjectives used to describe this supposed fact concerning contemporary social relations are not explicitly derogatory, the atmosphere of the paragraph as a whole is distinctly—nay, poignantly—that of a lament. What clearly comes across is a deeply felt sadness and frustration before the impermeableness of the barriers between self and self—a despairing desire to merge the discrete and opaque personalities dictated by gesellschaft [social group held together by impersonal relationships] and to enter a state of communal knowledge and even communal being. Reflecting upon the ironclad separation of souls within the "great city" may indeed provoke wonder and awe—but it also clearly elicits a wish that things might be otherwise.

The imagery employed in the passage is also pertinent if we remember that the working title of *A Tale* was "Buried Alive," for the passage continually attempts to blur the distinction between life and death, presenting a portrait of urban existence as a kind of living entombment. Not only does the incommunicability of souls have "something of the awfulness, even of Death itself . . . referable" to it, but the narrator, in his quest for closer communion with his fellow beings, speaks of himself as looking into "depths" for "glimpses of buried treasure." Furthermore, the deaths of his friend, neighbor, and love are described as "the inexorable consolidation and perpetuation" of their isolated, living states—as if these people are most true to their nature only after they have ceased to breathe. The final sentence, in which the corpses in actual graveyards are declared to be "sleepers" no more "inscrutable" than the town's "busy inhabitants," completes the equation of the living community with that of the dead. What the narrator has accomplished here is graphically to portray the "great city" as a metropolis in which everyone is virtually "buried alive": to depict a condition of society in which each citizen goes about his everyday offices—and even endures his supposedly most intimate moments—enclosed in a sarcophagus of impenetrable individuality. As we shall see, this damning critique of the way we live now inaugurates the subversive subtext which runs beside and beneath the narrator's subsequent denigration of the French Revolution's insistence that collectivities must supersede the individual as the fundamental unit of social life; it is here that we can apprehend the first movement of that counter-current which dares to consider the ideology of the Jacquerie as a possible escape from the "solitary confinement" mandated by bourgeois individualism. . . .

Dickens Distrusted Individualism

Dickens's novel of the French Revolution follows *Little Dorrit* in his canon, and much has been written about what attracted the author to a subject which, on the face of things, seems rather distant from his usual literary milieu. Of course we have Dickens's own words in the preface explaining how he "conceived the main idea of the story" while acting in [Wilkie] Collins's *The Frozen Deep*. The similarities between the central dramatic conflict of the play and the novel, however, tell us little as to why he chose to set his work mainly in revolutionary Paris—after all, one may sacrifice oneself for a loved one and a rival in any number of possible situations. And then too, there is the problem of covering ground already pronounced upon—there is no other word for it—by his friend and mentor Carlyle. The obsequious tone of the preface, in which he states that "it has been one of [his] hopes to add something to the popular and picturesque means of understanding that terrible time" while simultaneously assuring us that "no one can hope to add anything to the philosophy of Mr. Carlyle's wonderful book" betrays the awkwardness and risk inherent in his project. I would suggest that it is possible the Revolution attracted him precisely because it allowed him to study, confront—and to some extent flirt with—modes of thought which claimed to offer a solution to what he perceived to be one of the pervasive diseases of his own society. To understand how clearly he did in fact see the endemic and secretive individualism which underlay his acquisitive culture as a blighting phenomenon, we need only glance back as far as his preceding novel. As Arthur Clennam [a character in *Little Dorrit*] walks the streets of London, his thoughts give rise to images which, as George Levine says, "speak with remarkable appropriateness as representative both of the plot(s) of *Little Dorrit* and of the texture of its world." Notice again how in this passage, as in Sydney's case [referring to the character Sydney Carton in *A Tale of Two Cities*], opacity of character is inseparable from acquisitive activity—how nefarious economic practices are protected by the obscuring partitions which mask self from self:

> As he went along, upon a dreary night, the dim streets by which he went seemed all depositories of oppressive secrets. The deserted counting-houses, with their secrets of books and papers locked up in chests and safes; the bankinghouses, with their secrets of strong rooms and wells, the keys of which were in a very few secret pockets and a very few secret breasts; the secrets of all the dispersed grinders in the vast mill, among whom there were doubtless plunderers, forgers, and trust-betrayers of many sorts, whom the light of any day that dawned might reveal; he could have fancied that these things, in hiding, imparted a heaviness to the air. The shadow thickening and thickening as he approached its source, he thought of the secrets of the lonely church-vaults, where the people who had hoarded and secreted in iron coffers were in their turn similarly hoarded, not yet at rest from doing harm; and then of the secrets of the river, as it

rolled its turbid tide between two frowning wildernesses of secrets, extending, thick and dense, for many miles, and warding off the free air and the free country swept by winds and wings of birds.

We are back in the "great city" of the Night Shadows passage, the city from which barricaded Paris, whatever its barbarous cruelties, allows Carton, his author, and us a momentary escape. Dickens also writes in the preface to *A Tale*: "I have so far verified what is done and suffered in these pages, as that I have certainly done and suffered it all myself." After tracing [Jarvis] Lorry and Carton's well-disguised escapes from the constricting confines of bourgeois individualism, one understands better just how secretly liberating the "doing" part of Dickens's enterprise must have seemed to him, and how truly he bespoke his deep frustration with Victorian culture in calling the era of the Revolution both the best and the worst of times.

Class Divisions in Prerevolutionary France Mirrored Those in Victorian England

Nicholas Rance

Nicholas Rance is a literary critic. Among his works are Wilkie Collins and Other Sensation Novelists.

Charles Dickens makes two contradictory suggestions in A Tale of Two Cities, *states Rance in the following viewpoint. In the first, Dickens notes the similarities between prerevolutionary France and Victorian England and warns the British not to provoke revolution by oppressing the working class, Rance explains. The critic goes on to point out that Dickens believed the atrocities perpetrated in France were highly unlikely to occur in England due to the less violent nature of the English temperament.*

The [French] Revolution was painfully contemporary history for [Charles] Dickens: "I have so far verified what is done and suffered in these pages, as that I have certainly done and suffered it all myself." [Thomas] Carlyle's work [*The French Revolution: A History*], and that of the French historian [Jules] Michelet, were also composed in emotional turmoil. To Carlyle, the history was "a wild savage book, itself a kind of French Revolution", while Michelet interrupted his labours to inform a correspondent,

> I am accomplishing here the extremely tough task of reliving, reconstituting and suffering the Revolution. I have just gone through *September* and all the terrors of death; massa-

Nicholas Rance, "3: Charles Dickens: A Tale of Two Cities (1859)," *The Historical Novel and Popular Politics in Nineteenth-Century England.* Barnes and Noble Books, 1975, pp. 85–86, 94–101. Copyright © 1975 by Rowman & Littlefield Publishers, Inc.

cred at the Abbaye, I am on the way to the revolutionary
tribunal, that is to say, to the guillotine.

What Happened in France Had Implications for England

Still, the received version of the Revolution—that "awful, re-
pulsive cloud", detached from the world—allowed English his-
torians and historical novelists an escape from suffering. On
the one hand, the Revolution was vital prehistory, and Dickens must write a novel warning his generation not to provoke
the English sans-culottes [radical left-wing working class]. On
the other, it was an historical monstrosity, incapable of breeding. *A Tale of Two Cities* wavers between the two positions and
gradually settles for the more comfortable. In April 1855,
Dickens had written:

> I believe the discontent to be so much the worse for smoul-
> dering instead of blazing openly, that it is extremely like the
> general mind of France before the breaking out of the first
> Revolution, and is in danger of being turned by any one of
> a thousand accidents . . . into such a devil of a conflagration
> as never has been beheld since.

In 1857, he thought "the political signs of the times to be just
about as bad as the spirit of the people will admit of their being", and expected the next dose of cholera to make "such a
shake in this country as never was seen on Earth since Samson [biblical figure] pulled the temple down upon his head".
Dickens' subject was all too relevant to the age, and could not
be treated as an "inexhaustible study". Revolutionary mili-
tancy, once described, is abstracted from its antecedents: England has nothing to learn from a freakish occurrence, and
the novel's admonitory thesis is nullified. The opening pages
argue not only that late-eighteenth-century England was in
many ways very like prerevolutionary France, but also that
England has not changed much since. On the final page, the

prophetic Sydney Carton sees France "making expiation for itself", and the Manettes "peaceful, useful, prosperous and happy" in England.

Dickens takes refuge in the dogma of national characteristics. The English need not worry about revolutions in France because the French are the sort of people who are always having revolutions. . . .

Carlyle Influenced Dickens

Carlyle's views on the Revolution cannot be systematised. He was proud of his reputation as its most impartial historian, but there is more contradiction than impartiality. He criticises his predecessors for recording the Reign of Terror in hysterics, and then explains the Terror by commenting that in history as in nature, certain periods are covered over by "darkness and the mystery of horrid cruelty". The autonomy that the forces of madness come to exercise suggests Carlyle's awareness that the Revolution was generating its own momentum; and significantly, his loathing for the radicals grew as he wrote the book. Hedva Ben-Israel remarks of the historian William Smyth that "if contemporary conditions drove him to the study of the Revolution, it is even more obvious how much this study helped to formulate his political opinions and to intensify the process of his growing conservatism". The same is true of Carlyle, and also of Dickens in *A Tale of Two Cities*. For both, the experience of writing on the Revolution showed that their liberalism was not proof against the description of class war.

A Tale of Two Cities was published in 1859, twenty-two years after Carlyle's history. Dickens' letters show an urgency in their forebodings of civil conflict lacking in Carlyle's essays, and cannot be suspected of indulging in revolutionary prophecy to speed reform. Apprehension of the London sansculottes was one reason why his account was remoter than Carlyle's from the historical actuality of the French Revolution. Defensively, and more than his mentor, he too missed the collective life or aim and saw only individuals. Though Carlyle diverts attention immediately afterwards, during the storming, his eye is on the Bastille:

> At every street-barricade, there whirls simmering a minor whirlpool,—strengthening the barricade, since God knows what is coming; and all minor whirlpools play distractedly into that grand Fire-Mahlstrom which is lashing round the Bastille.

Whole sentences in *A Tale of Two Cities* are very close to Carlyle, except for Dickens' more profound inclination to subordinate the historical event to the illumination of private character. His narrative of the storming concentrates not on the Bastille, but [Ernest] Defarge:

> As a whirlpool of boiling waters has a centre point, so, all this raging circled round Defarge's wine-shop, and every human drop in the caldron had a tendency to be sucked towards the vortex where Defarge himself, already begrimed with gunpowder and sweat, issued orders. . . .

The Crowd Becomes a Force of Nature

Dickens the novelist might seem to be realising the Revolution through its impact on the individual, but he rather implies that Defarge is the guiding force of the Revolution. The conversion of Carlyle's vibrant metaphor to a laboured simile suggests the difficulty with which Dickens dramatised his dubious version of events. The revolutionary crowd which is active in Carlyle ("whirls simmering", "play distractedly", "lashing") is acted upon in Dickens. Consistently, Carlyle's irony is subdued to the hysteria of the individual as victim, the novelist's response to his projection into the past. Madame Defarge's Bacchantes [raucous intoxicated revolutionaries] substitute for the "one woman (with her sweetheart), and one Turk" who, according to Carlyle, joined the sans-culottes in storming the Bastille. The dialogue is bizarre throughout the novel, but Madame Defarge says some extraordinary things because she is a mad puppet talking to herself; she enjoys the splendid isolation which is [Charles] Darnay's, when he crosses to Paris during the Terror in the hope of restraining the revolutionary fury. Amongst the crowd, Defarge is as helpless "as if he had been struggling in the surf at the South Sea": even the arch-instigator is estranged from the struggle at hand. The idea of the crowd as a natural force is narrowed down until emphasis falls only on the cruelty of nature, and the history becomes increasingly deterministic, helping Dickens to draw his generalised moral about revolutions.

Dickens Sees Similarities Between France and England

In the opening pages of *A Tale of Two Cities*, Dickens sees little to choose between the condition of prerevolutionary France and that of England in the late eighteenth century; or of England in the 1850s. [James] Fitzjames Stephen's review missed the point by implying that the automatic sneer at the past was characteristic of the novel, despite the odd hint of Victorian complacence. Commonly derived from the French Revolution was the lesson of what happened when a country's aristocracy abjured its responsibilities and ceased to govern, and reviewing [Alexis de] Tocqueville's account in the *Edinburgh*, W.R. Greg found a picture "of that destruction of all *class cohesion*—that dissolution of the entire nation into a mere crowd of unconnected units—which made the convulsion, when it did come, utterly unopposed and irresistible. . . ." Dickens' England in the 1780s is precisely a "crowd of unconnected units", with no one playing a defined social role. "The highwayman in the dark was a City tradesman in the light", and the ease of the transition suggests a resemblance between the two occupations. The social fabric, so far from being settled forever, is ripe for violent change.

At this point, Dickens is not merely attacking harsh rulers who ought to be more charitable. For Carlyle in *Chartism*, democracy was "the consummation of No-government and *Laissez-faire*" [doctrine opposing governmental intervention in economic affairs]. In the novel [*A Tale of Two Cities*], Jerry Cruncher thinks of his occupation and tells himself, "you'd be in a Blazing bad way, if recalling to life was to come into fashion. . . ."; but as well as being a body snatcher, Jerry is also a messenger for Tellson's Bank, which equally would be in a bad way. The society trusting its wealth to Tellson's vaults provides dead bodies in plenty for Jerry to dig up again. The great keys of the underground strongrooms at Tellson's correspond to those of the Bastille; and as the Bastille is the symbol of oppression in France, so is Tellson's in England. Its broad social tendency is reflected in the depersonalisation of its employees: [Jarvis] Lorry's life is spent "turning an immense pecuniary mangle". Dickens hints that if oppression continues, there will be a storming of Tellson's, whose great keys will open the vaults for good.

Dickens Fears the Revolutionaries

Dickens' assault on the system of *laissez-faire* does not, however, survive his descriptions of revolution in France. He is induced to settle for any society that is non-revolutionary, forgetting that the old regime in England had seemed patently to invite revolution. Gradually, Lorry becomes an unequivocally positive figure; at first because, despite his disclaimers, he unites "friendship", "interest", and "sentiment" with banking. Later, Lorry's virtue is inseparable from his attachment to Tellson's. During the Revolution, he occupies rooms in the Parisian branch of the bank, "in his fidelity to the House of which he had grown to be a part, like a strong root-ivy". The root-ivy simile looks sinister, but the undertones conflict with Dickens' intended meaning, and are a confused remembrance of the days when Tellson's itself seemed a decidedly sinister institution. What Tellson's stands for in England is made plain after the outbreak of revolution, when the aristocratic emigrées flee there as to a natural haven. It is nevertheless at this stage that Dickens begins to approve of the bank. He has stressed that England has been brought close to revolution by political and economic reaction; yet when (for Dickens) a roughly similar state of affairs has provoked revolution in France, Tellson's can somehow be portrayed as a source of social stability.

Though the doctor has been victimised by the old regime in France, the Manettes' safety is linked with that of the money in Tellson's vaults, which is safe enough under Lorry's guardianship. They have not always enjoyed such security. The house in Soho had been "a very harbour from the raging streets", but Dickens associates the wreaths of dust in Soho with those raised by the Parisian sans-culottes. Gradually, he identifies with that British orthodoxy regarding the Revolution as "the one only harvest ever known under the skies that had not been sown", a random occurrence bearing no warning for England. He continues to state that the Revolution is the product of intolerable oppression, but the tale moves in another direction. The career of Miss Pross is significant. Her chauvinism begins as a joke, more John Bullish than the articles on France in *Household Words*. When she asks why providence should have cast her lot in an island if she was intended to cross the sea, Dickens is being gently satirical; less gently, he satirises those claiming their social rank from providence. But at the end of the novel, in the woman-to-woman struggle with Madame Defarge, Miss Pross's chauvinism is justified: her courage is specifically English, "a courage that Madame Defarge so little comprehended as to mistake for weakness". Miss Pross becomes an agent of the derided providence, and writing to [Edward] Bulwer[-Lytton] in 1860, Dickens gravely defended her enemy's "accidental" death.

> Where the accident is inseparable from the passion and action of the character; where it is strictly consistent with the whole design, and arises out of some culminating proceeding on the part of the character which the whole story has led up to, it seems to me to become, as it were, an act of divine justice.

Miss Pross literally harbours Lucie Manette from the raging streets. Embodied in Madame Defarge, the Revolution derives less from oppression than French depravity, which is no match for English virtue.

At the beginning of the novel, Dickens sees the Revolution as a rebuff to middle-class ideology. His scorn for the mentality (Lorry's) vindicating business as "a very good thing, and a very respectable thing", is reminiscent of Carlyle's strictures on the limitations of the Girondins [a political faction in France]. But Dickens cannot sympathise with the actual revolutionaries whom he portrays, and tells us why in his account of Madame Defarge:

> ... the troubled time would have heaved her up, under any circumstances. But, imbued from her childhood with a brooding sense of wrong, and an inveterate hatred of a class, opportunity had developed her into a tigress.

Madame Defarge can be excused for being revolutionary in a general kind of way, but not for her class ideology, whose violence provokes a corresponding violence in Dickens. The blood-smeared eyes of the sans-culottes sharpening their weapons in Tellson's yard are "eyes which any unbrutalised beholder would have given twenty years of life, to petrify with a well-directed gun". "Unbrutalised" reads ironically, and there is more irony if we remember the petrified Monseigneur. Dickens now prefers the stony hearts of the aristocracy to the revolutionary crowd, and would play the Gorgon [fearsome creature of Greek mythology] with history as the French aristocrats tried to do.

Early in the novel, since the ruling class has reneged on its responsibilities, virtue is not a connotation of fine dress. Dickens' later tendency, to assume that clothes make the man, derives from the persuasion that nations must be composed of unconnected units, each one a "profound secret and mystery to every other". Dickens becomes indignant with revolutionary innovations. From the look of the tribunal, he comments, it would seem that "the felons were trying the honest men". The moral order turned upside down will be that wherein "honest" justice is meted out to felons; presumably the judicial norm in non-revolutionary society. Darnay has contrary experience of the English bench. Oddly, though, he recoils from the aristocrats in La Force [a French prison] through an "instinctive association of prisoners with shameful crime and disgrace". Sympathy with the victims of revolution leads Dickens to share with [Charles] Darnay the conventional prejudice which has been invalidated.

Carton's Prophesies Are Overly Optimistic

Sydney Carton's career is problematic: He is clearly a failure, but Dickens sometimes seems to be asking whether in such a society as Carton finds himself, it is not a virtue to be a failure. While he may be simply weak, "the man of good abilities and good emotions, incapable of their directed exercise", the kind of strength leading to success is exemplified in Stryver:

> anybody who had seen him projecting himself into Soho while he was yet on the Saint Dunstan's side of Temple Bar, bursting into his full-blown way along the pavement, to the jostlement of all weaker people, might have seen how safe and strong he was.

Tellson's strongrooms are also "safe, and strong, and sound, and still"; and the stillness here is an emblem of the ultimate stultification of Stryver's bustling activity. Stryver's success as a lawyer is based on the exploitation of the weak Carton, while his own contribution to the partnership is to be "glib", "unscrupulous", "ready" and "bold". These business virtues combine with a resentment of democratic movements threatening to jeopardise his opulent living, and at Tellson's, he broaches to the emigrées his plans for "blowing the people up and exterminating them from the face of the earth. . . ." Stryver's disposition towards the French revolutionaries is shared by Carton as he ceases to be the mere jackal. While Madame Defarge points him to the National Palace, Carton reflects that "it might be a good deed to seize that arm, lift it, and strike under it sharp and deep". In the face of revolution, Carton is as willing to resort to repressive brutality as any *homme sensible* [sensible man], and his progressive ennoblement in the novel cannot be dissociated from his acquisition of bourgeois traits. Yet once, Carton had been seen not only as weak (that is one explanation), but also as among the numerous victims of a ruthlessly competitive society. "And whose fault was that?" asks Stryver, when Carton complains of his failure. Carton feels that it was Stryver's, whose "driving and riving and shouldering and pressing" forced his partner to a self-preserving "rust and repose".

Carton also competes, unsuccessfully, with Charles Darnay for the love of Lucie Manette, and his pining for the middle-class doll undercuts his subversive potential from early on. It is implied that his failure in love is inevitable, but the pining over Lucie is not convincing: There are qualities in the Carton who talks back to Stryver which suggest more backbone. Perhaps, and without slighting Lucie, Dickens was hinting that domestic content depended on worldly fortune; and that in the society he was treating, this was not for everybody. Lucie rejects Stryver, too, while Darnay is the happy medium: undoubtedly successful, but earning his modest income conscientiously as a private tutor. What is important in Carton's case is that the rebel should die at the hands of the revolutionaries on behalf of Lucie and the middle-class family, and if the situation seems contrived, that is all to the point. Anyway, the enigmas of Carton's career—the strained progress from rebel to revolutionary victim, and the dubious values which accompany his ennoblement—are shelved at his death, along with other problems which the historical novel has raised, not always intentionally. If Carton has been corrupted within history (as Dickens may have sensed), his death is a comprehensive retreat from the world's stain. As the guillotine falls,

> the murmuring of many voices, the upturning of many faces, the pressing on of many footsteps in the outskirts of the crowd, so that it swells forward in a mass, like one great heave of water, all flashes away.

At the end, Carton prophesies a secure and happy England without relation to the England presented earlier; nor, one would have thought, did the France of 1859 merit his optimism.

Dickens's Theme Is Resurrection

It is the passivity of the future state which is insisted upon, and Carton's death is the logical consummation of a novel increasingly stressing the blessings of inertia as the Revolution proceeds. Activity (movement in history) is associated with corruption, passivity with preserved innocence. Lorry, praised as the best possible man "to hold fast by what Tellson's had in its keeping, and to hold his peace", is beyond criticism because he refuses to enter the historical argument. History begins with the Fall, the collapse of timeless innocence, and the Carmagnole [a street dance popular at the time of the French Revolution] is "emphatically a fallen sport": but as the dance passes, leaving Lucie frightened and bewildered, "the feathery snow tell as quietly and lay as white and soft, as if it had never been". Quietly, the snow obliterates the marks of history, and returns the world to a uniform white. This, rather than the fallen historical world of Madame Defarge, is Lucie's habitat. Before becoming respectable, Carton called her a doll; accurately since, although Lucie marries and has several children, she never acquires a character. Throughout, she enjoys the immunity to time which England offers her at the close.

To state mechanically what is mechanically executed, the theme of resurrection pervades the novel. Dr [Alexandre] Manette is saved from burial alive in the Bastille, but has gone mad, and needs Lucie's loving care to revive his senses. Darnay is twice rescued by Sydney Carton from what seems certain death, in London and Paris, and Jerry Cruncher is a "Resurrection-man", or body snatcher. There are two mock funerals, those of Cly, the Old Bailey spy, and Foulon [referring to French politician Foulon de Doué], who causes a servant to be buried in his stead and is "recalled to life" only to be slaughtered by the Parisian crowd. Resurrection suggests a possible moral resurgence, and early in the novel, the idea of that resurgence is inseparable from social change. Dickens is curiously honest about Dr Manette's second resurrection, the restoration to mental health. "In a mysterious and guilty manner", Lorry hacks to pieces the shoemaker's bench, while Miss Pross holds the candle "as if she were assisting at a murder": their secret destruction seems like "a horrible crime", but the patient cannot be cured otherwise. Lorry's and Miss Pross's demolition of the mementoes of the Bastille precedes its razing by the revolutionaries.

Later in *A Tale of Two Cities*, destruction and secrecy are simply wicked. Resurrection assumes exclusively Christian connotations, and as Carton prepares to die to save Darnay, the words of the Anglican burial service recur to his mind. The Christian position is the same as Carlyle's in "Signs of the Times": "to reform a world, to reform a nation, no wise man will undertake; and all but foolish men know, that the only solid, though a far slower reformation, is what each begins and perfects on *himself*". Dickens is forced to such modest wisdom through his fear of revolution in England, and yet in a way he is still being honest. Carton yearns less for resurrection than the "far, far better rest". Finally, the escape from history is enough.

The Revolutionaries
Are No Better than the
French Aristocracy

George Woodcock

George Woodcock was a Canadian travel writer, poet, essayist, historian, professor, and biographer. His best-known book is Anarchism: A History of Libertarian Ideas and Movements. *A* Tale of Two Cities *was written during a tumultuous period in Charles Dickens's life and reflects the author's darkening worldview, states Woodcock in the following viewpoint. Marxist critics are incorrect when they claim Dickens as a revolutionary author, Woodcock maintains. Rather, Dickens believed that the violence of the revolutionaries was just as destructive as the oppression by the French aristocracy, he argues. The real answer for Dickens, Woodcock concludes, was for individuals to behave with decency and a spirit of brotherhood.*

The decision to choose revolutionary France as his setting [for *A Tale of Two Cities*] was undoubtedly the fulfillment of an intent which [Charles] Dickens had long harboured. Almost twenty years before, in 1840, he had first met Thomas Carlyle, and had fallen immediately under the spell of that powerful writer and bizarre personality. The reading of Carlyle's *Chartism* and *The French Revolution* had already influenced Dickens in writing *Barnaby Rudge* (1840–41), and now it was the apocalyptic Carlylean vision of insurgent Paris that Dickens allowed to shape the setting and influence the tone of the novel he planned. He had read *The French Revolution* repeatedly since its appearance in 1839, and he found no book that was to be of greater use to him. . . .

George Woodcock, "Introduction," *A Tale of Two Cities* (Charles Dickens), Crown Publishers Inc.,1970, pp. 12–25. Copyright © 1970 by The Writers' Trust of Canada. All rights reserved. Reproduced by permission.

France Was Very Familiar to Dickens

There were also at his disposal the memories of his several visits to Paris during the preceding decade and a half. In 1845 he had talked there with the French historian of the Revolution, Jules Michelet; he met [novelist] Victor Hugo on several occasions, and knew the poet [Alphonse de] Lamartine and the socialist Louis Blanc, leading figures in the revolution of 1848, while in the winter of 1855–6 he saw a good deal of the newspaper editor, Émile de Girardin, who in 1848 had been locked in the Conciergerie, a prison noted in the annals of the earlier and greater revolution. Apart from what he learnt from these friends in France, Dickens could draw on popular memories of the Revolutionary and Napoleonic Wars that lingered in England into the 1850s; when he began to write *A Tale of Two Cities*, the Terror [the Reign of Terror, 1793–1794] was nearer in time than the Boer War is today [1970] and Waterloo was a mere forty-three years in the past. Yet he kept returning to Carlyle because Carlyle's ornate rhetoric suited his own cast of mind, and it was *The French Revolution* that remained his principal source, next to his own past.

Changes in Dickens's Personal Life Darkened His Worldview

The memories of that past were stirred by the series of dramatic personal events through which he lived as *A Tale of Two Cities* matured in his mind. For, while he prepared to write on a public revolution, Dickens experienced a private revolution in which all the circumstances of his life were changed. At last, in 1858, his marriage was fissured by an incompatibility between this mercurial and melodramatic artist and his phlegmatic and unimaginative wife, Catherine. At no time since their wedding in 1836 had Catherine been enough to fill Dickens's emotional demands; as soon as they married, her young sister Mary Hogarth went to live with them, and Mary's sudden death in 1837 filled Dickens with a grief that echoed

Portrait of actress Ellen Ternan, reputedly the mistress of Charles Dickens. © Hulton Archive/Stringer/Hulton Archive/Getty Images.

through his novels to the end of his life. Her place was taken by her sister Georgina, another young and vivacious girl who appealed to his romantic persona until in the 1850s, when she too was leaving her youth, her place in his feelings was taken by the young actress Ellen Ternan who had acted with him in [a play by Wilkie Collins] *The Frozen Deep*. There is no need to continue the controversy that has raged among Dickensians regarding the actual relations that existed between Dickens and Ellen Ternan; the important facts are, first, that once again Dickens fell under the emotional spell of a young girl, as he had fallen under those of Mary and Georgina Hogarth (and before them of Maria Beadnell), and, secondly, that the infatuation with a girl outside the Hogarth sisterhood was the immediate cause of his separation from his wife. Henceforward—whether or not he kept Ellen Ternan in a suburban cottage—his household was dominated by his sister-in-law Georgina, who remained loyal to him when her sister departed, and in this new atmosphere the tempo of his life increased until the last compulsive days of exhausting public readings precipitated his premature death.

At the same time as Dickens brought his marriage to an end, the restlessness that stirred him led to a break in his long-standing association with his publishers, Bradbury and Evans; not only did he take his books away from them and resume relations with Chapman & Hall, but he also killed the magazine, *Household Words*, which he had been editing for them since 1850. These changes in his personal life have an appearance of abruptness, but they represent the eruption into his life of long-building forces of inner change that had been evident in his novels since the publication of *Bleak House* in 1853, and which drove him to a far more sombre view of life and of his aims as a novelist than had been possible in the years between *The Pickwick Papers* and *David Copperfield*. The revolution that engulfed the characters of *A Tale of Two Cities* gave symbolic form to the revolution that had engulfed Dickens as a man and as an artist. At this point his vision was tragic, and no matter how he might apply the salve of humourous relief, thinly in *A Tale of Two Cities* or thickly in *Great Expectations*, the mood of his work was to remain so into the deepening shadows of *[The Mystery of]* *Edwin Drood.* . . .

A Tale of Two Cities Reflects Dickens's Past

A Tale of Two Cities contains within its many connotations the whole sweep of the author's vision. For the balancing of London and Paris, and their different ways of life and of politics, is not all the title suggests. It suggests the basic dichotomy on which the novel rests: the choice between changing society and changing ourselves; the gulf between revolutionary ideals and revolutionary methods. It suggests also the dualities within the human heart, externalized in the key relationship between [Charles] Darnay and [Sydney] Carton. . . .

As a historical novel in any literal sense, *A Tale of Two Cities* has obvious limitations. It attempts no really panoramic view of either the English or the French political world of those critical years; *Barnaby Rudge*, its precursor in the use of popular uprisings, was much more thorough in that respect. A single State Trial suffices to give us the tone of English public life under George III; as for the Revolution in France, only two actual episodes are taken out of history and re-enacted in the novel, the fall of the Bastille and the lynching of 'old Foulon' [referring to French politician Foulon de Doué], and in both Dickens follows Carlyle very closely. None of the great personalities of the Revolution comes on the scene, and only the executioner Samson is mentioned among them.

Where Dickens did take hints from life in shaping his characters, they were derived from personalities who played extremely minor roles in history. The first spark of the revolutionary wine merchant [Ernest] Defarge seems to be found in the scanty reference Carlyle makes to a real wine merchant, Chôlat, who led the amateur *canonniers* [gunners] at the Bastille and took charge of the escort which failed to save

[Bernard-René Jordan] De Launay, governor of the fortress, from the rage of the populace. The germ of Dr Manette was undoubtedly contained in the prisoner, Queret-Demery, whose letter, begging the man who has imprisoned him for news of his wife, provides the pathetic note on which Carlyle ends his account of the fall of the Bastille. And it has been said that Stryver, the bullying, bombastic lawyer who thrives by picking Carton's misused brain, was based on Edwin James, Q.C., a mid-Victorian barrister whose courtroom style Dickens had witnessed on a single occasion. But Defarge, Stryver, and even Dr Manette, are secondary characters; the figures in the centre stage, Darnay, Carton and Lucie [Manette], have their sources within Dickens; they are the products of self-projection, of transmuting memory, and in part of a half-reasoning, half-intuitive conception of the moral destiny of man.

Dickens can be seen, in an image no more fanciful than his own, as a kind of Mahomet [character in the play with the same name by Voltaire] suspended between a dreaded but unforgettable past and a bright but unlikely future, and the material he selects from life is determined largely by these preoccupations. He is a didactic writer, with lessons to teach as to how men may live more decent and more Christian lives. But he is also a man who has not outlived the traumas of youth, which recur from novel to novel. One can see this double pattern in the way Dickens chooses to portray France and its revolution. Just as we realize that the Paris he creates is like no historical Paris, and quite unlike the Paris he knew on his own visits there during the 1840s and 1850s, so we learn quickly that the revolution which occurs in this fantasy city is dark with the shadows of his own past, and dominated by preoccupations inherited from his childhood.

Imprisonment and Injustice Are Motifs

The first is with imprisonment. Dr Manette is immured in the Bastille under the Bourbon regime; Darnay first appears as a prisoner in the dock at the Old Bailey, and later, under the new dispensation in France, he is shut up in La Force and the Conciergerie; Carton becomes a voluntary prisoner. The novel begins and ends with the opening of prison doors, even if, for Carton, they open only on to death.

There is no need to search deeply for the source of this preoccupation. Dickens bore as a deep emotional scar the memory of his father's detention for debt in the Marshalsea prison. It was a wound to his childhood pride which he never forgave society, and never forgave his father, for he linked it with the fecklessness with which John Dickens allowed his son, educated for better things, to spend the most wretched months of his childhood working in Warren's blacking factory. The looming memory of the prison experienced in childhood never left Dickens, and from *The Pickwick Papers* to *Great Expectations* his novels contain prisons and fathers or father substitutes immured in them. In *A Tale of Two Cities* the imprisoned father appears in dual guise: as Dr Manette at the beginning, and as Darnay (the father of little Lucie) at the end. In a hidden way each imprisoned father is also a delinquent father. Dr Manette deserts his family when he dares to write to the Minister exposing the Marquis's crime; and Darnay does the same when he goes to France (without even telling Lucie beforehand) to rescue the postmaster [Théophile] Gabelle from the guillotine.

Linked with the images of the prison and the delinquent father is the sense of an injustice never assuaged. 'In the little world in which children have their existence, whoever brings them up,' says Dickens in *Great Expectations*, 'there is nothing so finely perceived and so finely felt, as injustice. It may be only a small injustice the child can be exposed to; but the child is small; and its world is small.' As the child grows, its world expands, and so, if it has not been dispelled, does the sense of injustice, until it erupts in dreams of violence, and the mob attacking the Bastille, or in *Barnaby Rudge* in burning Newgate, becomes the fulfillment in fantasy of a child's anger.

Dickens Was Obsessed with Violence

This brings us to Dickens's second preoccupation in representing the French Revolution. It is the obsession—the word is hardly too strong—with destructive violence. Significantly, the violence that fascinates and horrifies him most is not that of the revolutionary state—embodied in the guillotine—but the violence of the mob, of the populace whose long-suppressed rages are suddenly released. There is no single instance in the novel in which we are shown the guillotine in action, though there is a great deal of bloodthirsty talk about it on the part of the Defarges and their companions. Even in the last scene, as Carton awaits execution, it is only a whirring and thudding monster which he hears behind his back. This restraint is particularly significant since, while Dickens had never seen a French mob in action, he *had* been present at a guillotining, in Rome in 1845, and had described it with an objective eye to detail combined with a disgust at the indifference of the spectators to the sickening spectacle. Yet he never put this experience to use in *A Tale of Two Cities*, while he did construct horrifying scenes of mob violence out of second-hand accounts imaginatively transmuted.

The vision which such scenes represent of destructive forces latent in society had been with Dickens for a long time. If one reads *Barnaby Rudge* and *A Tale of Two Cities* together it is evident that, though twenty years divide them, though they concern different uprisings in different countries with different intents, the passions of the mobs which rampage through them are virtually identical. The feeling of lapsed humanity, of the upsurging of all that is bestial and evil and irrational within man, is evoked equally strongly in both novels, though the way of expression significantly differs. . . .

Revolution Was the Result of Repression

Dickens is not seeking, in describing the actions of the mob with such vigour, merely to enjoy vicariously the liberating destruction they unleash, though in one self he is there, dancing among them, destroying prisons and taking revenge for the injustices of childhood. He is also, as a novelist, writing about events that still had meaning in the 1850s for a Europe plagued by threats of revolution, seeking the cause of such events in the depths of society and the hearts of men. His conclusion is clear, and two lines of [W.H.] Auden summarize it admirably:

> Those to whom evil is done
>
> Do evil in return.

Not only does he show the men and women who committed the worst atrocities during the French Revolution to have been—like Darnay and Lucie—good fathers and mothers and lovers, with a natural though undeveloped sense of the social virtues. He also argues clearly and definitely that the French nobility sowed the whirlwind that destroyed it.

It is this recognition that the Revolution was the natural and perhaps inevitable consequence of social oppression continued over centuries that has led the Marxist critics, such as T.A. Jackson and Jack Lindsay, to treat *A Tale of Two Cities* as a work of revolutionary intent, and to claim Dickens as one of their own. It is true, of course, that Dickens has always been a favourite author among revolutionaries and radicals. [Karl] Marx and [Friedrich] Engels both appreciated his novels and regarded him as in some degree a fellow fighter in the war against the social abuses of Victorian England. Rebels as assorted as [G.K.] Chesterton and [George] Orwell have written on him with intelligence and gusto, recognizing a temperamental affinity.

Dickens Was No Revolutionary

But the revolutionaries—if not the rebels—are deceiving themselves when they proclaim Dickens to be of their opinion. The violence of the Revolution, he maintains, is as negative as the oppression of a rigid social order, and just as self-destructive. The members of the mob in *Barnaby Rudge* turn from destroying property to killing themselves, and Defarge in *A Tale of Two Cities* is marked as a victim of the guillotine he serves. The Revolution repopulates the prisons, and no prospect could have seemed more repellent or more anti-human to Dickens. Madame Defarge is the ultimate personification of the Revolution in *A Tale of Two Cities*, and she is a being whom the uncontrolled desire for revenge has turned into a monster of pure evil. The final struggle between her and Miss Pross is a contest between the forces of hatred and of love. It is love that wins, when Madame Defarge in her turn is self-destroyed, through the accidental discharge of her own pistol. . . .

In fact, if Dickens had a lesson to teach his time in *A Tale of Two Cities*, it was to be spoken only in moral terms. He regarded violence as the necessary end of violence; prison as the consequence of prison; hatred as the wages of hatred. He preached that we must not allow society to take on the condition of frustrated anger in which men become mobs and the world is violently upturned. . . .

The important point is that Dickens realized such dangers could not be removed by repression, by more hangings or more imprisonment, but only by recognizing and alleviating the conditions that caused them. In one of his few political speeches, criticizing the Palmerston government [referring to the government of Viscount Palmerston of the Whigs] in 1855 for its conduct of the Crimean War, he declared that one of the tasks he had sought to fulfill as a man of letters was 'to understand the heavier social grievances and to help to set them right', and in another speech of the same period he declared that 'literature cannot be too faithful to the people—cannot too ardently advocate the cause of their advancement, happiness and prosperity'.

But this did not make him a revolutionary. It was not a change in the shape of society that he sought. He had no programme for an ideal society, and brought forward very few constructive suggestions of any kind; essentially what he criticized were the wrong moral attitudes, the attitudes that allow social abuses to accumulate out of selfishness or mental lethargy, and, as Orwell has pointed out, 'in every attack . . . upon society he is always pointing to a change of spirit rather than a change of structure'. Of politics and politicians he had been as sceptical as the anarchists ever since his employment as a reporter in the House of Commons, and he was content to see piecemeal changes brought about by the spread of education and by peaceful persuasion, provided they emanated from a proper sense of human decency and human brotherhood. Even within *A Tale of Two Cities* the alternatives to the fatal cycle of oppression and upheaval are present. If all French noblemen had been as willing to abandon their privilege as Darnay; if all French intellectuals had been as willing to expose abuses as Dr Manette; if all men were as willing to make sacrifices for their fellows as Sydney Carton; if there were more kindness like Mr [Jarvis] Lorry's, or more love like Pross's, or more loyalty in a tight corner like Jerry Cruncher's; then, we are expected to assume, the world would be a far better place, in which revolutions would no longer take place and prisons would not be built for men to be buried in.

The Theme of *A Tale of Two Cities* Is Resurrection

It is in fact by a moral resurgence that Dickens hopes to defeat the threat of revolution, and the idea of such a resurgence is clearly linked with the theme of resurrection that permeates every level of *A Tale of Two Cities* and assumes an almost grotesque variety of forms. . . .

So richly does Dickens elaborate [the] theme of resurrection, and the related theme of renunciation, both inherited from *The Frozen Deep*, that one is bound to suspect that the very persistence with which the idea of 'recalling to life' is brought to our attention may conceal a deeper and perhaps an opposing theme. The suspicion is justified. That other theme is death.

We return to the trio who hold the centre of the luridly il-luminated stage, and to their links with their creator. Lucie is not derived directly from Maria Beadnell or Mary Hogarth or Ellen Ternan, but she projects that yearning which appeared as regularly in Dickens's novels as it did in his life, towards the pristine femininity of vivacious young girls. She does not de-velop or change as the story progresses, even though she be-comes a wife and several times a mother, because Dickens wants her to remain perpetually young and perpetually—in spirit—a maiden. Romantically, the maiden is associated with death.

That takes us into the realms of the Gothic sensibility, and nothing is indeed more Gothic than the framework in which Dickens presents Carton and Darnay. They are doubles, alike in appearance, loving the same maiden, linked by fate. It is because he is Darnay's double that Carton can rescue him from the Old Bailey and give his life for him in Paris. The two doubles are linked also in their relationship with their creator. Steven Marcus has pointed out the revealing 'alphabet game' which Dickens plays with the names of his characters, endow-ing them with his own initials, from David Copperfield, through [Arthur] Clennam and [William] Dorrit in *Little Dorrit* and [James] Carker and [Paul] Dombey in *Dombey and Son*, to Carton and Darnay in *A Tale of Two Cities*. Dar-nay not only possesses both of his creator's initials, but shares his Christian name as well, yet he is not complete without the linking of surnames to which Carton is essential.

Darnay represents the light, sunny, optimistic aspect of Dickens's literary persona; this is shown especially by the way in which, on receiving Gabelle's plea for help, he sets off to

Paris without anticipating the perils he may encounter. He is the most unconvincing character in *A Tale of Two Cities*, as shallow as a mirror.

It is essential to the literary convention of the double that the two people involved, even if they do not represent respectively good and evil, should at least represent light and dark. Carton is Darnay's darkness, and, for that matter, Dickens's darkness. He is a kind of lesser Lucifer, a fallen brightness, dedicated to debauchery, prostituting his gleaming intelligence to the service of the unspeakable Stryver. He loves Lucie, but at first denies her (he terms her—with crushing accuracy—a 'golden-haired doll') and then fails to claim her. When he chooses death, it is not as heroes do in the prime of vibrant life, but when he has already abandoned all hope of a meaningful existence. Before he dies physically, he has already died in spirit. He sacrifices himself, not for Darnay's sake, but for Lucie's, and because he has no hope of her.

Seen in the context of the other later novels of Dickens, and of the last sombre years of their creator's life, the death of Carton can be detached from the platitudes with which *A Tale of Two Cities* ends. They, like the ending to *Great Expectations*, were a sop to the reading public of the 1850s. Carton, consistently developed, would not have looked 'sublime and prophetic at the guillotine'; he would not have thought optimistic thoughts of the future. He would, in accepting the death he had willed for himself, not only have fulfilled one deep longing of his creator, but also have died in the spirit of the world in which Dickens enclosed him, the world of the Revolution, for whose most striking personifications, the Defarges, there was no question of resurrection.

A *Tale of Two Cities* Depicts a Professional Class in Transition

Simon Petch

Simon Petch is a senior lecturer in the Department of English at the University of Sydney.

Although the British lawyer Sydney Carton is a central figure in A Tale of Two Cities, *many critics disagree as to his role in the novel, states Petch in the following viewpoint. The critic suggests that Carton's nationality and profession are significant. In contrast to the French physician Alexandre Manette, who is forced to take up a trade at one point in the novel, Carton is depicted as effective and independent, Petch suggests. Through this contrast, Dickens is suggesting that the British bourgeois system of the Victorian era holds more promise than the French system either before or after the Revolution, Petch concludes.*

A *Tale of Two Cities* is the story of one lawyer, Sydney Carton, and his self-sacrificing love for one woman, in the context of his relations with several other professional men, at the time of the French Revolution. It is also the most problematic novel in the [Charles] Dickens canon, primarily because of the elusiveness of its hero, the barrister Sydney Carton. We know, from what Dickens said about his own performance as Richard Wardour in Wilkie Collins's *The Frozen Deep*, that Carton was central to the emotional genesis of A *Tale of Two Cities*, and most readers would agree with Richard M. Myers: "Carton is the pivotal figure in the *Tale*, not merely because of the central importance to the plot of his

Simon Petch, "The Business of the Barrister in A Tale of Two Cities," *Criticism*, vol. 44, no. 1, Winter 2002, p. 27. Copyright © 2002 by Wayne State University Press. All rights reserved. Reproduced by permission.

heroic suicide, but because he embodies all the disparate elements of the novel's moral-political drama." But there is little agreement about Carton's precise place in this drama. Those who read *A Tale of Two Cities* as an historical novel find Carton difficult to pin down because he is such an apparently ahistorical figure, and feminist or gender-based criticism has subtended Carton's function to that of the female characters. Thus Hilary Schor dubs the novel "a Tale of two Daughters" and maintains that Carton functions for Lucie [Manette] as "the guide to the erotic wanderings that mark (off) the adulterous path." Other commentators have responded to his elusiveness by casting him in a variety of roles—Byronic hero [romantic hero named after Lord Byron], Carlylean hero [heroic leader named after Thomas Carlyle], even as a clown in a harlequinade [a pantomime with a harlequin and a clown]. As Albert D. Hutter has said: "[Carton] suffers chronically from meaning too much in relation to too many other characters and themes."

Law Is Central to *A Tale of Two Cities*

Despite his centrality to the novel's plot, Carton is an "unsubstantial" social presence, on the edge of groups to which he belongs only tangentially, and at home nowhere. In [Charles] Darnay's first trial, before Carton's decisive intervention, his attention is "concentrated on the ceiling of the court," and his torn gown and untidy wig may—for all we know at this stage—suggest professional incompetence. The narrator handles Carton with figurative delicacy: after a night's work with Stryver, Carton is "rumoured to be seen at broad day, going home stealthily and unsteadily to his lodgings, like a dissipated cat," a simile which intrigues because of the indirection with which it is approached ("rumoured to be seen"), and which tells precisely because Carton is not returning from a night on the tiles, but from a working night that has set his partner up for the day's legal battles, and which therefore hints at Carton's own problematic involvement with his work. As "the jackal" to Stryver's lion, Carton metaphorically provides his senior barrister with professional sustenance. But the jackal, in [evolution theorist Charles] Darwin's words, is "an animal not destined by nature to exist[,] & carrying with it the provision for death." Such a symbolically hybrid form perfectly captures Carton's morbid alienation, which drives him unpredictably between self-hatred and self-pity.

[James] Fitzjames Stephen's celebrated trashing of this novel was prompted by a lawyer's anger at the novelist's misrepresentation of legal process, but his hostility at least has the virtue of drawing attention to the centrality of law in Dickens's conception of his novel. At the opposite end of the critical spectrum perhaps only a lawyer might claim, as the barrister Edward Clarke did in 1914, that "the one great heroic character to be found in the works of Charles Dickens is Sydney Carton." These legal opinions chart the parameters of this essay, which explores the significance to the novel of Carton's status as a barrister. And, following critics who have looked beyond Carton's obvious doubling with Darnay to his more complex connections with his senior barrister Stryver, with Alexandre Manette, and with Jarvis Lorry, I examine Carton in the context of the professional culture that is integral to the representation of English society in *A Tale of Two Cities*.

The novel's treatment of French and English cultures of work is unbalanced. In France, the novel shows us the aristocracy of the ancien régime [prerevolutionary social and political system] in exploitative relation to the peasantry and the urban working classes; in England neither aristocracy nor peasantry is represented, the only lower class worker is Jerry Cruncher, and the focus is firmly on middle-class professional males—the lawyers Stryver and Carton, the businessman Lorry, and the tutor Darnay. Alexandre Manette, Doctor of Beauvais, is the significant French connection, linking the two cities of the title, in both of which he works, and also comparing, through his working lives, the professional cultures of France and England.

England and France Are Contrasted

The opening chapter of *A Tale of Two Cities* introduces the first of the many comparisons between France and England that pervade the novel: "There were a king with a large jaw and a queen with a plain face, on the throne of England; there were a king with a large jaw and a queen with a fair face, on the throne of France"; and both pairs of rulers, in 1775, "carried their divine rights with a high hand." But from this superficial similarity there emerges a contrast, as the chapter goes on to illustrate the defective legal system of each country. The example here offered of French injustice is the excessive punishment of a youth for failure to observe religious formality, an excess which prompts the narrative voice into a prophetic mode introducing the Woodman, Fate, and the Farmer, Death; in the logic of revolution, necessity is fomenting retribution. Dickens's sense of legal injustice in the England of 1775 is less systematic, but more complex, and more expansive, and in describing how the indiscriminate application of capital punishment to a variety of offences has created an ineffectual system of criminal justice, the narration is charged with comic energy:

> Daring burglaries by armed men, and highway robberies, took place in the capital itself every night; families were publicly cautioned not to go out of town without removing their furniture to uphoslterers' warehouses for security; the highwayman in the dark was a City tradesman in the light, and, being recognised and challenged by his fellow-tradesman whom he stopped in his character of 'the Captain', gallantly shot him through the head and rode away; the mail was waylaid by seven robbers, and the guard shot three dead, and then got shot dead himself by the other four, 'in consequence of the failure of his ammunition': after which

the mail was robbed in peace; that magnificent potentate, the Lord Mayor of London, was made to stand and deliver on Turnham Green, by one highwayman, who despoiled the illustrious creature in sight of all his retinue.

This carnivalesque catalogue of burglary and robbery dwarfs the single—and simple—French example of transgression, and in the irony which, throughout the passage, is directed at legal institutions, the narrative voice virtually celebrates such lawless anarchy. Richard [M.] Myers has said that in this chapter "Dickens describes France from the point of view of [Karl] Marx or [Jean-Jacques] Rousseau, and England from the point of view of [Thomas] Hobbes;" certainly, the critique of each legal system is shaped from a different ideological perspective. The most striking difference is that, in England, the criminal subculture underwrites the official economy: "the highwayman in the dark was a City tradesman in the light." Its energies may have been misapplied, but England in 1775 was a busy place, and this malfunctioning vibrancy is preferable to the France of the ancien régime, which, because all creative energy is stifled by oppressive authority, does not work.

Business Is a Recurring Motif

France is a worked rather than a working country because its labor is geared to aristocratic consumption rather than communal production. The aristocracy is represented in the person of Monseigneur, "one of the great lords in power at the Court," who requires not only a cook to prepare his chocolate, but also four "lacqueys" to serve it. This superfluity of servants is a synecdoche of a crisis of labor in French culture; it heralds the description of the mis-married Farmer-General and his overloaded retinue, which in turn foreshadows the diagnosis of disorder in the professions: "Military officers destitute of military knowledge; naval officers with no idea of a ship; civil officers without a notion of affairs; brazen ecclesiastics, of the worst world worldly . . . all totally unfit for their several callings. . . ." Integral to this "leprosy of unreality" is the sacrificing of "public business" to such nepotism and patronage; and several phrases—"sound business," "uncomfortable business," "anybody's business"—replay adjectival variations on one of the novel's key terms of reference, "business." In the reader's first, dramatic glimpse of France, after the wine cask smashes on the stones in Saint Antoine, as "All the people within reach had suspended their business, or their idleness, to run to the spot and drink the wine," the parallel clauses suggest equivalence, in France, between "business" and "idleness." After the Revolution, "business" in France fares no better, as can be seen from the career of the Parisian wood-sawyer, formerly a provincial mender of roads. The mender of roads is introduced as a bystander in the lead-up to the Revolution, as, "cap in hand," he is an incidental informant to Monsieur the Marquis. Drawn to Paris, this "provincial slave" is swept up in the Revolution, and transfers his servitude to [Ernest] Defarge and his wife. Planted in Paris near La Force [a prison], his earlier role as informer is intensified, and this "lacquey" of the Revolution masquerades as the wood-sawyer who observes Lucie's walks near the prison as she tries to let her husband see her. His insistent disclaimer, "'But it's not my business'" is revolutionary doublespeak, for such surveillance is entirely and specifically his "business." Rehearsed as a witness by Madame Defarge, the wood-sawyer later declares himself willing to manufacture such evidence—to perjure himself—as may be needed to convict Lucie. Such sinister "business" is a revision of the earlier parasitical "business" of the ancien régime, and a sure sign that the Revolution has bred its own sickness: plus ca change [the more things change]. "Business" is therefore a decisive term in the novel's analysis of French society, and, introduced by Jarvis Lorry, the self-styled "man of business," in the fourth chapter of the novel, it also serves to distinguish between the working cultures of England and France. The term "business" does suggestive work in the England of *A Tale of Two Cities*, where it becomes a site of ideological stress, and it is brought into particular focus through Sydney Carton. . . .

Professional Identity Is Significant

The Carton we see in court is very good at his job. . . .

The nature and quality of Carton's commitment to his professional identity give him an authority that is denied most of the professional men in *A Tale of Two Cities*. He is the touchstone by which the other professionals are judged, and so the central figure in the novel's masculine network of professional affiliations which may be traced from character to character through contrast, comparison, and mutual definition. Darnay, who lacks professional accreditation, is in this respect the shadowy double of Carton the renegade professional whose skills are acknowledged only by exploitation. At Cambridge, Darnay read with undergraduates as a sort of "tolerated smuggler who drove a contraband trade in European languages," an illicit trader relegated, like Carton, to the margins of the professional economy, but whose professional integrity, like Carton's, is impeccable. Carton and Stryver are contrasted as lawyers, and as suitors, "The Fellow of Delicacy" and "The Fellow of No Delicacy." Stryver's declaration to Jarvis Lorry of his intention to make an offer of marriage to Lucie Manette establishes a tension between "the banker" and "the barrister" that undermines the wall which Lorry is forever trying to build between his business character and his private relationships. When Darnay presses his suit for Lucie to her father, he strategically points out the similarities between himself and Dr Manette—"like you, striving to live away from [France] by my own exertions"—as voluntary exiles and independent professionals. And, ironically, it is Lorry's loyalty to Tellson's Bank that finally compels Darnay to go on his mission to France. His primary reason for going is to rescue the old servant [Théophile] Gabelle, but he finally overcomes his "latent uneasiness" and hesitation by "the pointed comparison of himself with the brave old gentleman in whom duty was so strong."

Manette's Professional Status in France Is Fragile

The most subtle filaments in this network of professional relationship and influence are those which link Carton with Alexandre Manette, and with Jarvis Lorry. Carton and Manette speak directly to each other only once in the novel. After Darnay has been condemned to death, Carton, his plan to rescue Darnay now fully formed, gets Manette out of the way by sending him back to the authorities for a final appeal. Manette and Carton seem unconscious of each other, and yet the novel silently builds bridges between them. Carton, like Manette, possesses a "useful life laid waste," and Manette's "black brooding" reflects the dark side of Carton. In the famous Night Shadows passage, the intriguing sense of the secrets of personality and the mysteries of individuality is equally proleptic of Carton and Manette. Like Manette, Carton is recalled to life through being reawakened to his professional identity.

Manette links France and England, and also contrasts the France of the ancien régime with republican France, but his professional status is the key to his complex function of the novel. Five years after his release from the Bastille, Manette earns a comfortable living in Soho: "Doctor Manette received such patients here as his old reputation, and its revival in the floating whispers of his story, brought him. His scientific knowledge, and his vigilance and skill in conducting ingenious experiments, brought him otherwise into moderate request, and he earned as much as he wanted." His capacity to control his income is the mark of his professional independence, and the dining room appropriately doubles as Manette's consulting room, for his work puts the food on the table. But this independence is illusory, and the profession is precariously perched over a trade, for in his bedroom his shoemaking bench and tools of that trade that he brought with him from prison in France await his dream life; the profession represses the trade, as the doctor represses the Bastille prisoner. On his return to France, Manette is most fully recalled to his professional life, a "new life" that is quite unlike his private practice in London. Appointed inspecting physician of three prisons at the age of sixty-two, Manette acquires a new and elevated status: "Silent, humane, indispensable in hospital and prison, using his art equally among assassins and victims, he was a man apart." And yet his status as the dignified and impartial epitome of professional public service is underwritten by his status as the Bastille captive; for what preserves Manette as "a man apart" is partly "the story of the Bastille captive," which "removed him from all other men." Because his present authority is grounded in his having been a prisoner of the ancien régime, Manette is still a prisoner; his professional authority is hostage to the republic, and, as becomes clear at his son-in-law's second French trial, his independence is politically contingent. The Revolution catches up with him: addressed as Citizen Doctor at the arrest of Darnay, at the trial he is plain Citizen Manette, without professional status, power or influence.

Manette's story, as completed by his own account of his dealings with the Evrémonde brothers, is a fable of professional disempowerment. Daniel Duman has claimed that in nineteenth-century England "the professions" developed into "a distinct and self-conscious social category," central to which "was the formulation and diffusion of a unique ideology based on the concept of service as a moral imperative." This was partly effected by the social and economic changes consequent upon industrialization: "The traditional bonds which connected the professions to the landed aristocracy began to loosen. The patron-professional relationship of the eighteenth century, in which the professional practitioner was dependent upon aristocratic custom, was replaced by a client-professional relationship." Manette's attempt to resist such "traditional bonds" sees them tighten around him, and his account of how a "young physician" with "a rising reputation" was betrayed and imprisoned, is an emblem of the injustice that inspired the Revolution. Hijacked in Paris by the Evrémonde brothers, he is assured that his "clients" are people of condition; but his "patients" are people of no condition, and this fissure between client and patient is the essence of a system of patronage of which Manette is as much the victim as the sister and brother of Madame Defarge. The term "Doctor" becomes highly charged in the several manners of its application. The dying boy consistently addresses Manette as "Doctor," whereas the Evrémonde brothers do not; in fact he is only addressed as "Doctor" by the elder brother when he is effectively threatened: "'Doctor . . . [y]our reputation is high, and, as a young man with your fortune to make, you are probably mindful of your interest. The things that you see here, are things to be seen, and not spoken of.'" The threat (heralded by acknowledgment of professional status, but enforced by the mention of "interest" and "fortune") is ignored by Manette, whose response—"'in my profession, the communications of patients are always received in confidence'"—reasserts a crucial distinction, and amounts to a refusal of patronage. Money is thrown, offered, given (but not taken), and then left at Manette's door. To accept payment from the brothers would obviously compromise Manette's professional status, because the money is a bribe for silence, and therefore complicity, rather than payment for service. Manette returns the money, and complains to the authorities, only to be betrayed by the minister to whom he writes, because the state is at the mercy or behest of the nobility—the pervasive condition of patronage that was analyzed so scathingly in "Monsieur the Marquis in Town." But at the trial of Darnay, the law is at the behest of the revolutionary tribunal, which results in a perversion of justice parallel to Manette's imprisonment. Working for the republic is little different from working for the ancien régime, and it is impossible not to contrast Manette's two periods in France with the true professional independence he acquires in England. Furthermore, the fortunes of his son-in-law in France anticipate the appropriation of Manette's identity by the revolutionary authorities. When Darnay sets foot in France his identity is immediately under siege, and the narrator's neutral designation "traveller" is translated, by the institutionally pressured speech of those running the Revolution, from "emigrant" to "aristocrat" to "prisoner." His name shifts with his status, and by the time he has reached Paris, Darnay has become Evrémonde. At Beauvais, ironically, Darnay learns of the decree that has made him a "traitor"; and the narrator's analogy for Darnay on his way to prison secures him in the economy of revolution, which will later engulf his father-in-law: "that a man in good clothes should be going to prison, was no more remarkable than that of labourer in working clothes should be going to work."

France and England Have Different Cultures of Professionalism

The contrast between French and English cultures of professionalism partly explains why Manette and Carton, who would seem to have much in common, have so little to say to each other in the novel. But this novel may also reflect the different degrees of independence enjoyed by the two professions of law and medicine in England. Duman maintains that during the late eighteenth and the early nineteenth centuries the bar and physic "represented two distinct types of professions and professionalism. The bar had begun to emerge as a proto-modern profession, a precursor of mid-nineteenth-century developments, while physic largely conformed to the paradigm of the pre-industrial gentlemanly professions. The physicians lacked complete autonomy over the content and goals of their work and discipline. The bar, on the other hand, had the independence and authority which resembled that later created by the new model professsions." While, at the time represented by the novel, both barristers and physicians worked largely for the landed classes, the relationship of the two professions to the social elite was by no means identical, for the barrister was less reliant upon "a particular geographical or social milieu" for his clients. The barrister's increasing liberation from aristocratic patronage was mirrored in the increasing diversification of his clientele, a process accelerated by the Industrial Revolution. And patronage, either by the aristocracy or the republic, is what contains Manette's independence and controls his professional authority in *A Tale of Two Cities*. This consciousness of what Duman has termed "the era of professionalism" (the second quarter of the nineteenth century) may have enabled Dickens to discriminate among the relative degrees of independence of the various professional occupations represented in the novel, and as an English advocate Carton is more of a free agent than Manette, the Doctor of Beauvais. It is significant that the hero of a novel written in 1859 should be an independent English professional. . . .

The relationship of professions and trades is uncomfortable in *A Tale of Two Cities*. . . . This is part of a broader interest in the relationship of work to social function which runs throughout the novel. The treatment of such concerns serves to contrast England and France, for whereas the economy of labor in France is geared to dysfunctional exploitation, in England the quality of the malfunctioning itself signifies energy in need of redirection. Sydney Carton points the way. Alienated from the exploitative competitiveness of capitalism, yet committed to professional service, he is himself the "live sign" of English bourgeois social ideology in 1859 (a year which saw the publication of Samuel Smiles's *Self-Help*, as well as of *A Tale of Two Cities*). As an independent professional and representative of the ideology of service, Carton symbolizes the potential for function that characterizes Dickens's critique of English society.

Nation and Generation in
A Tale of Two Cities

Albert D. Hutter

Albert D. Hutter was an associate professor of English at the University of California, Los Angeles.

In A Tale of Two Cities, *Charles Dickens explores the related themes of class conflict and generational conflict, suggests Hutter in the following viewpoint. These themes reflect Dickens's concerns with both social and psychological issues, Hutter explains. In Dickens's England, Hutter asserts, authority and repression are privatized and internalized, becoming a more psychological than political conflict and spurring extended conflict between fathers and sons. Hutter also argues that Dickens's emphasis on style and the technique of "splitting" results in oversimplification of rich historical subjects.*

Two revolutions, one generational and the other political, determine the structure of *A Tale of Two Cities*. We require a combination of critical methods—literary, psychoanalytic, historical—to illuminate the novel's complex structure and its impact on different readers. Lee Sterrenburg writes that [Charles] Dickens' vision of the French Revolution may be influenced by "a personal daydream only he can fully fathom. But he is able to communicate with his readers because he has rendered his daydream in terms of a publicly meaningful iconography." Since *A Tale of Two Cities* is also a tale of two generations, the iconography of father-son conflict carries a particularly powerful social resonance.

Albert D. Hutter, "Nation and Generation in A Tale of Two Cities," *PMLA*, vol. 93, no. 3, pp. 448–450, 452–453, 455–456, 458. Reprinted by permission of copyright owner, the Modern Language Association of America.

Dickens' novel was published in 1859, a year that Asa Briggs calls a "turning point" in the "late Victorian revolt against authority." This revolt originated "in mid-Victorian society. What happened inside families then influenced what happened in many areas of public life later." The major publications of 1859, from [Charles Darwin's] *The Origin of Species* and [Karl] Marx's *[A Contribution to the] Critique of Political Economy* to Samuel Smiles's *Self-Help*, stand poised between the anticipation of a later ideological revolt and the still powerful memory of the French Revolution. That revolution and subsequent English social reform inevitably changed Victorian father-son relations. But the changing Victorian family, in turn, reshaped society. As much as any other work of 1859, *A Tale of Two Cities* demonstrates the correlation between family and nation, and it uses the language of psychological conflict and psychological identification to portray social upheaval and the restoration of social order.

Nation and generation converge in the earliest chronological event of *A Tale of Two Cities*, Doctor [Alexandre] Manette's story of the Evrémondes' brutality (III, (X, 303–15). The Evrémondes rape a young peasant girl, wound her brother, then summon Manette to treat their victims. When Manette tries to report these crimes, he is incarcerated in the Bastille. He writes a full account of his experience—damning the Evrémondes to the last of their race—and hides this personal history in his cell. [Ernest] Defarge finds the document and uses it as evidence against Charles Darnay, né Evrémonde. The events Manette describes, a microcosm of the larger narrative, trigger the major actions and reversals of the double plot. The rape itself implies social exploitation, a class-wide droit du seigneur [right of a feudal lord to have sexual relations with the bride of his vassal]. Conversely, one peasant's attack on his master anticipates the nation's reply to such abuse. The Evrémonde who raped the girl and murdered her brother will later run down a small child from the Paris slums, and as a result will be "driven fast to his tomb." The retaliation denied one peasant, a generation earlier, is carried out by the revolutionary "Jacques." Even the Paris tribunal at which Manette's story is read reflects a struggle between parents and children: Manette has condemned his son-in-law to death.

Class conflict here reveals a hidden psychological conflict that recurs throughout the novel. Manette is taken at night and forced to witness the aftermath of a violent sexual assault. His abductors have absolute power, and any knowledge of their activities carries grave risk: "The things that you see here," the Marquis warns young Manette, "are things to be seen, and not spoken of" (III, (x, 311). Violence and sexuality, combined with a mysterious nocturnal setting and a dangerous observation, suggest a primal scene. Such scenes arouse anxiety about being caught spying, and they invariably reflect parent-child conflict. The political significance of this drama intensifies its psychological meaning. Evrémonde's absolute power, for example, resembles the father's absolute power over his child. The novel's virtual obsession with spying, its comic subplot, and its descriptions of revolutionary violence all further suggest primal-scene fantasies. But if we mistake this primal-scene reading for a full explanation of the novel, we only succeed in isolating one meaning and subordinating the others. We could as easily argue that the dominant class struggle—not simply in the novel but in Victorian history—is being expressed through the powerful language of childhood trauma: the nation is symbolized by the family; a national and historical struggle is made particular, and particularly vivid, through a personal and psychological narrative. The two explanations are not mutually exclusive. But to integrate them we must first analyze the whole work and locate the reader's experience in the structure of the text itself. It can be shown that the psychological chronology of the *Tale's* plot, turning as it does on Manette's story, duplicates a psychological chronology common to the experience of most readers.

Manette's story is the narrative equivalent of a trauma: It recalls an event that precedes all the other action of the novel and organizes that action, although it is not "recovered" until quite late in the novel. Modern psychoanalytic theory recognizes the retrospective quality of trauma, the way in which the individual reconstructs his past life to conform with present conflicts and thereby invests a past event with significances—some of it real, often some of it imagined. Manette's document stands in a similar relationship to the larger novel: Within the structure of the *Tale* it acts like a traumatic memory, reliving the significant antecedent events of the entire plot at the climax of Darnay's second trial. The document reveals the combination of public and private acts that informs the narrative; it records the "primal scene" of the text itself. . . .

The novel is filled with spies, from a hero twice accused of spying, to the comic spying of Jerry Cruncher, Jr., on his father, to the spy Barsad and "the great brotherhood of Spies" who inhabit St. Antoine. Even the dead men, their heads on Temple Bar, remind us of "the horror of being ogled." And the novel closes with an obsessive parade of violence, the revolutionaries worshiping the guillotine and previewing its victims at mass trials.

Spying, like virtually everything else in this novel, has two meanings—one public, the other private. The official spies, like Barsad, are instruments of repression and representatives of the "fathers," the men in power. But in other contexts, like the Cruncher scenes, children spy on their parents. In both cases spying expresses the *Tale*'s dominant conflicts. Thus the Gorgon's Head witnesses much more than the murder of the Marquis: It sees the deadly struggle between two generations, which is climaxed by implicit filicide and patricide. Dickens anticipates the public murders of the Revolution while suggesting the private conflict of Charles Darnay through the subtle mixture of two plot lines. . . .

The British world of business offers a different, more pragmatic solution to father-son struggles. Samuel Smiles, a widely read apostle for the self-made man, speaks for a common British chauvinism when he contrasts England and France:

> ... [the English system] best forms the social being, and builds up the life of the individual, whilst at the same time it perpetuates the traditional life of the nation ... thus we come to exhibit what has so long been the marvel of foreigners—a healthy activity of individual freedom, and yet a collective obedience to established authority—the unfettered energetic action of persons, together with the uniform subjection of all to the national code of Duty.

This description integrates independent action and submission to authority. Because Dickens' France prevents such integration, unrestrained selfishness and anarchy tear the country apart. Although England has both unruly mobs and abundant selfishness, the British control the central conflict between sons and fathers, independence and authority. In a land of opportunity the individual submits himself to a generalized authority, which he then internalizes—at least according to Smiles and most other Victorians. The virtues of "promptitude," "energy," "tact," "integrity," "perseverance"—the whole list of ingredients in Smiles's recipe for success in business—involve the same psychological dynamic: turn external tyranny into internal censorship and control. *Self-Help* opposes external help. Patronage, money, support in any form inhibit imitating one's business "fathers" and, by struggle and hard work, repeating their success. Government itself is internalized: "It may be of comparatively little consequence how a man is governed from without, whilst everything depends upon how he governs himself from within. The greatest slave is not he who is ruled by a despot ... but he who is the thrall of his own moral ignorance, selfishness, and vice." The description fits Carton perfectly, at least until his conversion. Carton demonstrates his moral degeneration by willingly playing jackal to

Stryver's pompous lion. Their relationship in turn demonstrates the Victorian businessman's divided personality: He hopes to rise in the world but he must never become a "striver," particularly in a field like law, where one must appear unruffled, cool, above all a gentleman. Dickens' social insight is conveyed by caricature and specifically by a psychological division that embodies an enforced social separation, not unlike the two sides to [John] Wemmick in *Great Expectations*. . . .

The two cities of Dickens' *Tale* embody two very different public expressions of father-son conflict. In England, particularly in the world of business, repression is internalized: It becomes a psychological act rather than a political one. As public repression is diminished, internal aggression is brought under control, and the generation in power transmits its own authority—its own image—to those who follow. In France, political repression is much stronger, as is the political retaliation of the oppressed. Dickens distorted the reality of the French Revolution to fit precisely into this liberal vision of the causes of revolution (and the need for a prophylactic reform), exaggerating the brutality and repression of the ancien régime [prerevolutionary French society] and reducing the uprising itself to a nightmare of populist, radical reaction. Dickens' historical distortion clearly states the prevailing British liberal attitudes toward political repression and reform, toward the value of business and free enterprise, and, implicitly, toward the frequent, and frequently unconscious, struggle between fathers and sons throughout the century. . . .

Dickens' familial and political revolutions are expressed by his varied use of splitting throughout the novel, so that the theme of the work becomes as well its characteristic mode of expression. From the title through the rhetorically balanced opening paragraphs, Dickens establishes the "twoness" of everything to follow: characters are twinned and doubled and paired; the setting is doubled; the women . . . are split; the historical perspective is divided between an eighteenth-century event and its nineteenth-century apprehension. "Splitting" thus describes a variety of stylistic devices, particularly related to character development and plot. But "splitting" also has two important psychoanalytic meanings: a splitting of the individual (specifically, the ego) and a splitting of the object. That is, an individual may deal with a specific problem, relationship, or trauma either by dividing himself or by dividing the problematic "other" (parent, loved one). Splitting is a fundamental mode of psychological defense and a key concept in the development of psychoanalytic theory. It originated in a description of schizophrenia and is now recognized as a central mechanism of multiple personality; but it may also be part of a normal adaptive strategy for coping with any intense relationship.

Dickens manipulates both emotional conflict and its solution by "splitting" in the technical, psychoanalytic sense: His characters distance their emotions from an immediate, and disturbing, reality (thus [Jarvis] Lorry's remark to Lucie [Manette] about his lack of feeling or Carton's apparent ability to separate himself from everything except the "higher" emotions at the close); he divides a single ego into two (Carton/Darnay); and he splits the "object," allowing one person (Charles's uncle) to bear the brunt of the hero's hatred or aggression toward Charles's father. Conversely, Dickens' use of doubles may suggest, not splitting, but reunifying something once divided or divisible: the comic identification of Jerry, Jr., with his father or the larger movement between London and Paris, which connects seemingly disparate incidents and persons and ultimately unites the two plots. Even in the famous rhetoric of the opening, the balanced opposites suggest their own ultimate fusion. The use of splitting in a work this long is too varied and extensive to justify simple praise or blame— splitting is primarily a descriptive term—but it should clarify the understandably divided critical assessment of the novel.

[James] Fitzjames Stephen had originally called the book's tone "thoroughly contemptible," while Dickens thought it could be the best story he had written. Sylvère Monod makes a more balanced appraisal, noting the special intensity of the revolutionary passages but finding the origins of that intensity in a "personal interest" that breaks down the proper distance between author and subject. Monod at times seems to withdraw his approval, but he is simply reflecting the work's contradictory quality: "Few would refuse to admit that the *Tale* is very much a contrived product," he has recently written, "[or] that the contrivance is usually superb." In addition to citing the lack of sustained comedy in the novel, critics have complained about the contrivance and sentimentality of Carton's role and about Dickens' oversimplification of a complex historical event. I have suggested that the failed comedy of the Crunchers derives, in part, from a failure to control, or, sufficiently disguise, the primal-scene material implicit throughout the text. Dickens' historical oversimplification reflects, as we have seen, a merging of family and class struggles that was both characteristic and particularly problematic in the nineteenth century. Carton's role, both as a "double" to the hero and as a melodramatic scapegoat at the close, develops the dual conflicts of the novel; indeed, much of the sentimentality of Carton-as-Christ is derived from his conversion, via Lorry, into the good son and the good conservative. Carton's solution is that of any son—or class—that willingly accepts the pain or injustice inflicted upon it by parents or rulers, and such a solution is not particularly satisfying to most readers. In his peculiarly calm and heroic way, Carton stands for the ideals of conservative belief, in the family and the nation, but he finally assumes too many meanings and is required to connect too many threads of the novel. He suffers chronically from meaning too much in relation to too many other characters and themes and, like Manette's document, unites too many incidents; he becomes more strained as he becomes more important.

Other kinds of splitting in *A Tale of Two Cities* far more successfully project the text's central conflicts, precisely because they require no resolution. Dickens' caricature of the lion and the jackal, for example, exploits an inherent, unresolvable tension in his social subject. The division of labor between Carton and Stryver powerfully suggests not only Carton's divided self but the divided goals and morals of Victorian business. . . .

Edgar Johnson has written that "*A Tale of Two Cities* has been hailed as the best of Dickens's books and damned as the worst. It is neither, but it is certainly in some ways the least characteristic. . . ." This essay tries to show, on the contrary, that in *A Tale of Two Cities* Dickens is concerned with two connected themes that preoccupied him throughout his career: the generational and political conflicts he repeatedly expressed through the technique of splitting. However, because that technique is used so pervasively in *A Tale of Two Cities*, it makes the novel seem uncharacteristically concentrated in style and, at times, uncharacteristically strained or humorless. The novel's particular combination of individual psychology and broad social concerns thus accounts for its unique qualities, its intensity, and its failures. *A Tale of Two Cities* dramatizes two dominant conflicts of the Victorian age—and of our own.

Social Issues
in Literature

Chapter 3

Contemporary
Perspectives on
Class Conflict

There Is a Growing Perception of Strong Class Conflict in America

Rich Morin

Rich Morin is a senior editor at the Pew Research Center.

Americans believe that the conflict between economic classes is stronger than that between immigrants and native-born individuals, the old and the young, and blacks and whites, reports Morin in the following viewpoint. A Pew Research Center survey released in January 2012 found that two-thirds of American adults believe class conflict between the rich and poor is strong or very strong, a finding that increased by 19 percent from a similar study conducted in 2009, Morin states.

The Occupy Wall Street movement [a group protesting social and economic inequality, greed, and corruption] no longer occupies Wall Street, but the issue of class conflict has captured a growing share of the national consciousness. A new Pew Research Center survey [released in January 2012] of 2,048 adults finds that about two-thirds of the public (66%) believe there are "very strong" or "strong" conflicts between the rich and the poor—an increase of 19 percentage points since 2009.

The Growing Perception of Class Conflict

Not only have perceptions of class conflict grown more prevalent; so, too, has the belief that these disputes are intense. According to the new survey, three in ten Americans (30%) say there are "very strong conflicts" between poor people and rich people. That is double the proportion that offered a similar view in July 2009 and the largest share expressing this opinion since the question was first asked in 1987.

As a result, in the public's evaluations of divisions within American society, conflicts between rich and poor now rank ahead of three other potential sources of group tension— between immigrants and the native born; between blacks and whites; and between young and old. Back in 2009, more survey respondents said there were strong conflicts between immigrants and the native born than said the same about the rich and the poor.

Virtually all major demographic groups now perceive significantly more class conflict than two years ago. However, the survey found that younger adults, women, Democrats and African Americans are somewhat more likely than older people, men, Republicans, whites or Hispanics to say there are strong disagreements between rich and poor.

While blacks are still more likely than whites to see serious class conflicts, the share of whites who hold this view has increased by 22 percentage points, to 65%, since 2009. At the same time, the proportion of blacks (74%) and Hispanics (61%) sharing this judgment has grown by single digits (8 and 6 points, respectively).

The biggest increases in perceptions of class conflicts occurred among political liberals and Americans who say they are not affiliated with either major party. In each group the proportion who say there are major disagreements between rich and poor Americans increased by more than 20 percentage points since 2009.

These changes in attitudes over a relatively short period of time may reflect the income and wealth inequality message conveyed by Occupy Wall Street protesters across the country in late 2011 that led to a spike in media attention to the topic. But the changes may also reflect a growing public awareness of underlying shifts in the distribution of wealth in American society. According to the most recent U.S. Census Bureau data [2010], the proportion of overall wealth—a measure that includes home equity, stocks and bonds and the value of jewelry, furniture and other possessions—held by the top 10% of the population increased from 49% in 2005 to 56% in 2009.

Perceptions of the Wealthy

While the survey results show a significant shift in public perceptions of class conflict in American life, they do not necessarily signal an increase in grievances toward the wealthy. It is possible that individuals who see more conflict between the classes think that anger toward the rich is misdirected. Nor do these data suggest growing support for government measures to reduce income inequality.

In fact, other questions in the survey show that some key attitudes toward the wealthy have remained largely unchanged. For example, there has been no change in views about whether the rich became wealthy through personal effort or because they were fortunate enough to be from wealthy families or have the right connections.

A 46% plurality believes that most rich people "are wealthy mainly because they know the right people or were born into wealthy families." But nearly as many have a more favorable view of the rich: 43% say wealthy people became rich "mainly because of their own hard work, ambition or education," largely unchanged from a Pew survey in 2008.

Moreover, a recent Gallup survey found that a smaller share of the public believes that income inequality is a problem "that needs to be fixed" today than held that view in 1998 (45% vs. 52%). And when asked to rate the importance of various alternative federal policies, fewer than half (46%) say "reduc[ing] the income and wealth gap between the rich and the poor" is "extremely" or "very" important. In contrast,

Occupy Wall Street protesters march along Broadway in downtown Manhattan, New York, on September 17, 2012. In the photo, the group is protesting what they believe to be an unfair economic system in the United States. © Steven Greaves/Corbis.

more than eight in ten (82%) say policies that encourage economic growth should be high priorities.

Social Conflict in American Life

About two-thirds of the public say there are strong conflicts between the rich and the poor, and nearly half of these (30%) say these conflicts are "very strong." An additional 36% say these differences are "strong," while 23% view them as "not very strong." Only 7% say there are no conflicts between rich and poor Americans, while the remainder does not offer an opinion.

Three other historic social divisions are viewed as less pervasive or contentious. About six in ten (62%) say there are strong conflicts between immigrants and the native born, including 24% who characterize these disagreements as "very strong."

That represents a major change from the Pew Research Center survey conducted in 2009. At that time, a larger share

135

of Americans believed that there were more strong conflicts between immigrants and the native born than between rich and poor people (55% vs. 47%). Today, even though perceptions of disagreements between immigrants and the native born have increased by 7 percentage points in the past two years, this social divide now ranks behind rich-poor conflicts in the public's hierarchy of social flash points.

Two other social divides are viewed as less pervasive or intense. Fewer than four in ten (38%) say there are serious conflicts between blacks and whites, including 10% who see these conflicts as being "very strong." About a third say there are similar disagreements between the young and old (34%, a 9-point increase since 2009).

Income and Perceptions of Class Conflict

The perception that strong and growing conflicts exist between the economic classes is broadly held. Not only do those at the bottom rungs of the income scale agree that there are serious disagreements between the economic classes, but even those who are relatively well-off hold that belief.

Nearly two-thirds (64%) of all adults with family incomes of less than $20,000 a year report serious conflicts between the rich and poor—a view shared by 67% of those earning $75,000 a year or more.

Moreover, the perceptions of class conflicts have grown in virtual lockstep across all income groups since 2009, rising by 17 percentage points among those earning less than $20,000 and by 18 points among those making $75,000 or more.

The increase is slightly larger among middle-income Americans earning between $40,000 and $75,000. Among this group, the share who say there are strong class conflicts increased by 24 points, from 47% in 2009 to 71% in the latest survey.

Other Demographic Differences

Young people ages 18 to 34—the demographic group most closely associated with the Occupy movement—is more likely than those 35 or older to see "strong" conflicts between the rich and poor. According to the survey, more than seven in ten (71%) of these young adults say there are major disagreements between the most and least affluent, a 17 percentage point increase since 2009.

Baby boomers [those born between 1946 and 1964] ages 50 to 64—the mothers and fathers of the Occupy generation—are nearly as likely to say there are serious conflicts between the upper and lower classes; fully two-thirds (67%) say this, a 22-point increase in the past two years. Among those ages 35 to 49, more than six in ten (64%) see serious class conflicts.

While older adults are the least likely to see serious disagreements between the classes, the proportion who express this view increased from 36% two years ago to 55% in the current survey.

Women are more likely than men to say there are serious disagreements between the rich and poor (71% vs. 60%). In 2009, about half of all women (51%) and 43% of men said there was strong conflict between the classes.

Perceptions of Class Conflict Surge Among Whites

In the past two years, the proportion of whites who say there are strong conflicts between the rich and the poor has grown by 22 percentage points to 65%. That is more than triple the increase among blacks or Hispanics. The result is that the "perceptions gap" between blacks and whites on class conflict has been cut in half, while among Hispanics the difference has disappeared and may have reversed.

In the latest survey, the difference in the share of blacks and whites who say there are strong conflicts between rich and poor stands at 9 percentage points (74% for blacks vs. 65% for whites). In 2009 the black-white divide on this question stood at 23 percentage points (66% vs. 43%).

Among Hispanics, the gap has closed and may have reversed: In 2009, the share of Hispanics who said there were serious conflicts between the economic classes was 12 points larger than the share of whites (55% vs. 43%). Today, the proportion of whites who say there are serious disagreements is 4 percentage points greater than the share of Hispanics who hold the same view (65% for whites vs. 61% for Hispanics), though this difference is not statistically significant.

The Politics of Class Conflict

Democrats and political liberals are far more likely than Republicans [GOP] or conservatives to say there are major conflicts between rich people and poor people.

At the same time, in just two years the perceptions of class conflict have increased significantly among members of both political parties as well as among self-described independents, conservatives, liberals and moderates.

The result is that majorities of each political party and ideological point of view now agree that serious disputes exist between Americans on the top and bottom of the income ladder.

Nearly three-quarters of self-described Democrats (73%) say there are serious class conflicts, an 18 percentage point increase over those who said that in 2009. The increase among Republicans was about as large (17 percentage points); currently a majority of GOP partisans see serious conflicts between rich and poor.

Views of class conflicts increased the most among political independents, swelling by 23 percentage points to 68% in the current survey. Two years ago, fewer than half of all independents said there were major disagreements between the classes.

Similarly, perceptions of class conflict among ideological liberals increased by 23 percentage points to 79% in the past two years while rising less quickly among conservatives (15 points) or moderates (18 points).

How the Rich Got Wealthy

Americans divide nearly evenly when they are asked if the rich became wealthy mostly due to their own hard work or mainly because they were born into a wealthy family or had connections.

A narrow plurality (46%) believes the rich are wealthy because they were born into money or "know the right people." But nearly as many (43%) say the rich got that way because of their own "hard work, ambition or education."

The latest result is virtually identical to the findings of a 2008 Pew survey. It found that 46% of the public believed that riches are mostly the result of having the right connections or being born into the right family, while 42% say hard work and individual characteristics are the main reason the rich are wealthy.

These competing explanations of wealth are cited by roughly equal shares of all income groups. According to the latest Pew survey, 46% of those with family incomes of less than $20,000 a year believe that luck and connections explain most wealth, a view shared by 47% of those with family incomes of $100,000 or more.

In contrast, attitudes of Republicans and Democrats on this issue are mirror opposites of each other. Nearly six in ten Democrats (58%) say wealth is mainly due to family money or knowing the right people. An identical proportion of Republicans say wealth is mainly a consequence of hard work, ambition or having the necessary education to get ahead. Political independents fall in between: slightly less than half (45%) credit personal effort, while an equal share believe family circumstances or connections are the most likely explanation.

African Americans (54%) are more likely than non-Hispanic whites (44%) to see wealth as a consequence of family money or connections, a view shared by 51% of Hispanics. Women in the survey are slightly more likely than men to say wealth is the result of family or connections but these differences are not statistically significant.

Young people are significantly more likely than older adults to believe most wealth is due to family money or connections (51% for those ages 18–34 but 37% for adults 65 or older). However, the views of the "younger young"—those 18 to 25—differ significantly from those who are just a few years older.

According to the survey, less than half (47%) of those 18 to 25 say the rich are wealthy because of reasons other than personal effort or drive, or about equal to the proportion of those 35 or older who share this view. In contrast, a majority (55%) of those 26 to 34 say being born into a wealthy family or personal connections are the main reasons that people are rich.

Attitudes toward the wealthy—specifically, how the rich got that way—are somewhat correlated with views on class conflict.

According to the survey, those who believe the rich acquired their fortunes mainly through their own efforts are significantly less likely than those who hold the contrary view to say there are strong conflicts between the classes (60% vs. 72%).

Income Inequality Is a Serious Problem in America

David Schultz

David Schultz is a professor at Hamline University School of Business and the editor of the Journal of Public Affairs Education.

Class divides America, argues Schultz in the following viewpoint, noting the growing income gap between the richest and the rest of the population. At the root of this divide are fundamental arguments about the role of government, he contends. One side believes in free market capitalism while the other believes that government needs to make sure the needs of all citizens are met, he maintains.

A line in the sand of American politics is being drawn. It is a line that cut through Madison, Wis., last spring [2011] in the debate over unions. It is a line being cut through Wall Street over the role of banks and hedge-fund managers in destroying the American economy in 2008. And it is a line cutting through Washington, D.C., in Congress over how to produce jobs, regulate banks, reduce the deficit and debt, and provide health care to those who need it. That line is about class in America.

Class Divides America

There is a basic belief in America that we are all in it together. We are one big happy middle class where the interests of the rich and poor are not in conflict. Rising tides lift all boats, as [former president] Ronald Reagan used to say. There are no class conflicts in this world. That what is good for GM [automaker General Motors] is good for America, and that we live in a society where all of us can be winners with no losers in the economic marketplace. The promise of America is of a non-zero-sum game—some do not have to lose for others to win. The truth is far uglier.

America is a nation characterized by increasing class divides. In 2010 the census reports the richest 5 percent of the population accounted for 21 percent of the income, with the top 20 percent receiving over 50 percent of the total income in the country. This compares to the bottom quintile accounting for about 3 percent of the total income.

Congressional Budget Office research found that the income gap between the top 1 percent of the population and everyone else more than tripled since 1973. After-tax income for the top 1 percent increased by 281 percent between 1973 and 2007, while for middle class or middle quintile it increased by 25 percent, and for the bottom quintile it was merely 16 percent.

Looking beyond income to wealth, the maldistribution has not been this bad since the 1920s. According to the Institute for Policy Studies, in 2007 the top 1 percent controlled almost 34 percent of the wealth in the country, with half of the population possessing less than 3 percent. The racial disparities for wealth mirror those of income. Studies such as the Survey of Consumer Finances by the Federal Reserve Board have similarly concluded that the wealth gap has increased since the 1980s.

Record Numbers in Poverty

Social mobility in America has ground to a halt. A 2010 Organisation for Economic Co-operation and Development study found that social mobility in the United States ranked far below that of many other developed countries. Other studies, including those in 2005 and 2010 in the *Economist* similarly

A child counting money from her piggy bank. Studies show there is better than a 95 percent chance that children in the United States will not improve their social economic status in comparison to their parents. © AP Images/Anhony Devlin.

point to declining social mobility in the United States that makes it difficult for individuals to rise from one social economic status to a better one. In fact, there is better than a 95 percent chance that children will not improve their social economic status in comparison to their parents. Finally, the latest census figures point to a poverty rate in 2010 of 15.1 percent, representing a record 46 million people in poverty. The numbers are equally grim when one looks at women, children, and people of color in poverty—all record or near record numbers. Few really can move on up to live the American dream.

The reality is that America is a zero-sum game. There are winners and losers. What is good for corporate America is not benefiting most Americans, and it is increasingly clear that in simple terms the rich are getting richer, the poor poorer. The reality is, we are not all in it together and class divides America. We see the divide in where individuals live, what they eat, and the entertainment they consume. It is seen in who votes, runs for office, and in political contributions. It is reflected in our tax code, criminal justice system and educational opportunities.

Class exists. The problem is, few want to acknowledge it. And when someone talks of economic redistribution, bailing out homeowners and not banks, taxing millionaires, or blaming Wall Street and not the government for the economic problems that ail America, cries of class warfare are raised. Or worse—[Republican author and radio host] Herman Cain "McCarthyited" [a term meaning made unsubstantiated accusations, named after former US senator Joseph McCarthy] the Wall Street protesters as "Anti-American," invoking the ugliest of all political epithets to assail opponents.

Protests Are Symptoms

Yes, class conflict exists in America. Protests in Wisconsin over attacks on unions or on Wall Street to challenge the power of banks reflect this. But they are merely symptoms of the broader battle over a simple question: "Why government?" It is a debate over whether free market fundamentalism prevails as a means to provide order and declare winners and losers in America versus letting the government correct the imperfections and errors that capitalism has produced. It is between saying that the direction of the country is decided by "one dollar one vote" or by "one person one vote." It is a battle over whether the government serves the interests of corporations and the rich or the rest of us.

Class exists in America, as it does in all other nations of the world. Like it or not, there are diametrically opposed interests in this country and the real questions are whether the government and politicians should do anything about it and whose interests they should serve.

Income Inequality Is Not a Serious Problem in America

Kip Hagopian and Lee Ohanian

Kip Hagopian is a cofounder of Brentwood Associates, a California-based venture capital and private equity firm. Lee Ohanian is a professor of economics and director of the Robert Ettinger Family Program in Macroeconomic Research at the University of California at Los Angeles as well as a senior fellow at the Hoover Institution.

Those who claim that income inequality is a problem in America that should be addressed by a redistribution of wealth have misstated the facts and have come to a conclusion that would be damaging to the economy, argue Hagopian and Ohanian in the following viewpoint. They point to data showing that the United States has outperformed most nations in gross domestic product and standard of living to support their contention that middle-class as well as upper-class incomes have increased over the past twenty-nine years. Hagopian and Ohanian recommend that legislators turn their attention to improving the K–12 education system to better train youth to be competitive in an increasing global marketplace rather than changing the tax code.

In October 2011, the Congressional Budget Office [CBO] published a report, "Trends in the Distribution of Household Income Between 1979 and 2007," showing that, during the period studied, aggregate income (as defined by the CBO) in the highest income quintiles grew more rapidly than income in the lower quintiles. This was particularly true for the

Kip Hagopian and Lee Ohanian, "The Mismeasure of Inequality," *Policy Review*, no. 174, August & September 2012, with the permission of the publisher, Hoover Institution Press. Copyright © 2012 by the Board of Trustees of the Leland Stanford Junior University.

top one percent of earners. This CBO study has been cited by the media and politicians as confirmation that income inequality has increased "substantially" during the period studied, and has been used to support President [Barack] Obama's claim that income inequality is a serious and growing problem in the United States that must be addressed by raising taxes on the highest income earners.

We will show that much of what has been reported about income inequality is misleading, factually incorrect, or of little or no consequence to our economic well-being. We will also show that middle-class incomes are not stagnating; in fact, middle-class incomes have risen significantly over the 29 years covered by the CBO study. Lastly, we will address assertions that the rich are not paying their "fair share" of taxes.

In our view, Americans should care about the well-being of the nation as a whole rather than whether some people earn more than others. To that end, the focus of public policy should not be on equality of income but on equality of economic opportunity. Policies designed to reduce income inequality inevitably involve redistribution of income through increases in transfer payments and marginal tax rates. But these policies discourage hiring and investment, which depresses economic growth and opportunity. In sharp contrast, policies designed to enhance equality of opportunity will increase economic well-being for all, most particularly those in lower income households.

Income Inequality

Perhaps the most important question left out of almost every discussion about income inequality is, "Why should we care about it?"

Many of those who worry about high income inequality argue that it is an indicator of social injustice that must be remedied through redistribution of income (or wealth). Unfortunately, those who make this claim have not provided any generally accepted criteria for determining when an economic system is unjust. Nor have they provided a convincing argument that such injustice is widespread in the U.S. (In considering this issue, it is worth noting that Greece, Spain, and Italy all have substantially lower income inequality than the U.S. The same is true for Afghanistan, Pakistan, and Bangladesh.) . . .

An important shortcoming in the October 2011 CBO report is its almost singular focus on *income* as a measure of economic well-being, when there is a clear consensus among economists that the best measure of living standards *over the long term* is not income, but consumption. Focusing on consumption rather than income provides a very different picture of inequality.

There is a body of research indicating that consumption inequality is not only substantially lower than income inequality, but has been declining in recent years. . . .

[Consumption] inequality is considerably lower than income inequality. This is because consumption expenditures are made with after-tax dollars and are influenced by many factors other than money income, including transfer payments, family savings, barter, imputed rent from owner-occupied housing, income from the underground economy, and assistance from family and friends. . . .

Measuring Economic Well-Being

We believe the focus on income inequality is misguided. The most important finding of the CBO report is *not* that income grew more in the higher quintiles than in the lower quintiles; it is that income in *all* quintiles grew. And, as measured by the PCE [personal consumption expenditure deflator], incomes grew significantly faster than reported.

America's economy has outperformed all other industrialized nations. The vast majority of Americans have fared well over the period of the CBO study. In fact, the U.S. economy has been the best-performing large economy in the world as measured by per capita GDP [gross domestic product] and median standard of living. According to the OECD [Organisation for Economic Co-operation and Development], per capita GDP in the U.S. in 2010 was $46,600, which is 47 percent higher than the $31,800 average per capita GDP in the EU [European Union] nations in that year.

In addition to substantially higher GDP per capita, the U.S. has a significantly higher standard of living than almost all of the most advanced economies. According to "The Luxembourg Wealth Study," the data source used by the OECD for international comparisons, in 2002 (the latest year for which results were available), median disposable personal income in the U.S., adjusted to reflect purchasing power parity, was 19.3 percent higher than in Canada; 68 percent higher than in Finland; 45 percent higher than in Germany; 59 percent higher than in Italy; 31 percent higher than in Norway; 73 percent higher than in Sweden; and 31 percent higher than in the United Kingdom. . . .

Further evidence of the superior economic performance of the U.S. economy comes from a comparison of unemployment rates. The average unemployment rate in the United States from 1982 to 2007 was 6.0 percent, compared with 9.0 percent in France, 8.3 percent in Germany, and 7.7 percent in the United Kingdom.

The not-stagnant middle class. . . . The claims that incomes in the U.S. have been stagnant "for decades" are at odds even with the arguably understated income growth data from the CBO report, which show that income in the middle three quintiles grew "just under 40 percent." And as we have seen, using the PCE deflator, incomes in the middle three quintiles grew about 48 percent.

While these growth rates are somewhat below historical averages, they are impressive inasmuch as they occurred during a period of rapid globalization and technological change.

In any event, it is clearly wrong to say that middle-class income growth during the period was "stagnant."

America's poor: Putting poverty into perspective. Currently, about 46 million Americans live below the official federal poverty line. But the data suggest that by some measures America's poor have a somewhat higher standard of living than is commonly believed.

Based on a standard established in 1965, a family of four reporting $22,300 or less in money income in 2010 was considered poor and thus eligible for government support. By this standard, about 15 percent of Americans are currently judged to be poor, roughly the same percentage as was reported in 1965, and up from 12.5 percent before the recession. However, in his 2008 book *The Poverty of "The Poverty Rate,"* American Enterprise Institute [for Public Policy Research] scholar Nicholas Eberstadt makes a compelling case that the government measure for the "official poverty rate" is seriously flawed. His assertion is based largely on the fact that the reported income of people defined as poor has increased only about 10 percent since the standard was set, while other measures of well-being have increased substantially more.

Most notably, consumption expenditures by the lowest-income Americans have consistently exceeded reported income, and, this difference "has widened tremendously over the decades since the official poverty rate made its debut." Specifically, Eberstadt reports that according to the Department of Labor, in 1960–61 consumption expenditures in the lowest quartile were 112 percent of reported income, rising to 140 percent (in the lowest quintile) in 1972–73, and 198 percent (in the lowest quintile) in 2005. Thus, a family claiming $22,300 in income in 2005 would have reported about $44,000 in expenditures in that year. As noted earlier, the gap between reported income and consumption is filled by various categories of government transfer payments (including Medicaid, food stamps, subsidized housing, the earned income tax credit,

Temporary Assistance for Needy Families, etc.), family savings, imputed income from owner-occupied housing, barter, support from family and friends, and income from the underground economy. . . .

Why U.S. Income Inequality Is Higher

There does not appear to be a clear consensus among economists as to why inequality in the U.S. is higher than in other industrialized nations.

There are many factors that contribute to income inequality, at least two of which are common to all countries and are unalterable. They are: differences in individual ability and preferences (defined as the capacity and desire to earn) and differences in age (this latter factor is currently in evidence in the U.S., as 80 million aging baby boomers [those Americans born between 1946 and 1964] are passing through their peak earnings years). . . . A third influence on inequality in almost all countries during the last 30 to 40 years has been globalization.

In addition to these common factors, we believe there are several factors specific to America that have put upward pressure on income inequality. Some have enabled certain segments of the population to earn extraordinary incomes, and some have caused certain segments to lag behind.

Extraordinary incomes at the top. The most influential factors enabling the growth in incomes in the U.S. appear to be:

- Greater economic freedom. . . .
- A highly developed entrepreneurial culture. . . .
- The "electronics revolution." . . .
- A large, highly developed venture capital industry. . . .

Yes, these factors have combined to produce massive wealth for a few—but have also contributed to raising incomes for most.

Suppression of incomes at the low end. In addition to globalization and technology, another important factor putting downward pressure on incomes in the U.S. has been the substantial influx of low-skilled, low-income immigrants into the U.S. workforce over the past 30 years.

But as noted at the beginning of this [viewpoint], we and others believe that an even more important cause of lagging incomes in America is inequality of opportunity. There is considerable debate over what impedes equality of opportunity. Many assert that institutional racism and sexism is a major factor; others argue that the political system is rigged in favor of corporations and the rich. These explanations seem to have as many detractors as they have advocates. But one cause of lagging incomes on which there is broad agreement is America's substandard K–12 education system. We believe that a solution to this problem would do more to reduce income inequality and increase prosperity than any other public policy fix.

Have tax cuts increased inequality? A common claim is that the rate cuts for capital gains and dividends under President [Bill] Clinton together with President George W. Bush's cuts in marginal rates and further cuts in capital gains and dividend rates raised income inequality. But the evidence does not support that claim. . . . A plausible explanation for this is that the Bush tax cuts reduced taxes on people with lower incomes more than it did on people with higher incomes. For example, under Bush, the lowest marginal rate, 15 percent, was lowered to 10 percent (a 33 percent reduction), while the highest marginal rate, 39.6 percent, was lowered to 35 percent (a 12 percent reduction). In addition, under Bush, the child credit doubled and the earned income tax credit increased significantly, further reducing the tax obligations of lower income earners. This has almost certainly contributed to the increase in workers who pay no federal income tax, which now totals about 47 percent of tax filers. . . .

Do the Rich Pay Their Fair Share?

The answer to this question should start with an agreement on an accepted definition of fair. But those who assert that the rich do not pay their fair share have not provided such a definition. . . .

The U.S. income tax system is, by any measure, quite progressive. In fact, according to a study released in 2008 by the OECD, the U.S. federal income tax system is the most progressive of any of the 24 countries in the "OECD-24," which includes Canada, Japan, Australia, and all of the richest European nations: Germany, France, the United Kingdom, Italy, the Netherlands, Norway, Switzerland, Luxembourg, and Sweden. In fact, the U.S. progressivity index is 22 percent higher than the average for the 24 countries. . . .

Do higher income earners pay lower tax rates? The latest argument in favor of raising the taxes on higher income earners is that the rich pay lower average *rates* than lower income earners. This claim has been given currency by the famed investor Warren Buffett, who recently announced that he paid a lower rate of tax on his income than did his secretary. Since most of Buffett's income comes from dividends and capital gains (which are taxed at the rate of fifteen percent), and assuming Buffett pays his secretary well, it is understandable that the rate shown on his tax returns would be less than the rate paid by his secretary. However, the relationship between Buffett's low tax rate and that of his secretary is a statistical outlier. According to the CBO, the rich, on average, definitely pay higher income tax rates than lower income taxpayers.

Moreover, as the *Wall Street Journal* among others has noted, Buffett has ignored the fact that the taxes on corporate dividends and capital gains are taxes on corporate income that has already been taxed once at rates as high as 35 percent, not including state taxes. (Thirty-five percent is the statutory rate of tax on corporate income; the average rate is 25 percent.) . . .

So what is a "fair share"? The U.S. tax system is more progressive than that of any other advanced economy. Higher income workers already pay a substantially disproportionate amount of the income tax relative to their share of income. The top five percent pay 44 percent more in taxes than the bottom 95 percent, while 47 percent of tax filers pay no tax at all. The bottom 50 percent of filers pay only 2.3 percent of taxes, and the bottom quintile gets money back.

Based on these facts, how does one make a case that the rich are not paying their fair share?

Equality of Opportunity

We are unaware of persuasive evidence that reducing income inequality will increase economic well-being for the majority of citizens; in fact, America's superior standard of living and economic growth relative to other advanced economies is evidence to the contrary. For arguably the most commonly used measure of inequality and for the Census Bureau's most comprehensive definition of income, inequality has not risen since 1993. Moreover, the rise in income inequality that occurred before that year appears to have been, at least in part, a byproduct of the remarkable success of a group of entrepreneurs who in the past few decades created countless jobs and contributed substantially to the higher living standards we all currently enjoy.

Increasing taxes on America's most productive earners—those who create most of the jobs in our economy—will depress economic growth and reduce opportunities for the less fortunate. Rather than focusing on income inequality, policy makers should address the very real impediments to achieving equality of opportunity, particularly for the youngest and least-skilled workers among us. We believe such efforts should begin with fixing our K–12 education system, which is failing to train many young Americans to be competitive in today's global labor market. If we can solve this problem, we will enable future generations of young people to climb the economic ladder and achieve the economic success that has long made the United States the world's leading economy.

Globalization, Technology, and the Rising Value of Education Are Creating Income Inequality

Steven J. Markovich

Steven J. Markovich contributes to the Council on Foreign Relations' Renewing America blog.

Income inequality is on the rise in America, and globalization, technological change, the rising value of education, and changes in tax rates are among the factors contributing to its growth, contends Markovich in the following viewpoint. Class mobility has stalled, with more than 40 percent of those born into the lowest income class doomed to stay there, the author claims. The tension caused by income inequality is likely to result in political conflict, Markovich concludes.

In September of 2011, the Occupy Wall Street protests [demonstrations against social and economic inequality, greed, and corruption] began in New York and quickly spread across the globe. Its "We are the 99 percent" slogan encapsulated popular angst over income inequality that had been rising steadily over the years. Today, inequality in the United States, measured by the standard Gini coefficient [the most commonly used measure of inequality], is substantially higher than almost any other developed nation, and even some developing countries such as Russia and India.

While income inequality can be summarized in a few words, its multiple potential causes are more complex. Globalization and technological change have simultaneously led to greater competition for lower-skilled workers—many of whom have also lost union membership—while giving well-educated, higher-skilled workers increased leverage. Changes to tax rates, including favorable treatment for capital gains, may also play a role.

Rising U.S. Income Inequality

Income inequality in the United States has been rising for decades, with the top echelon of earners rapidly outpacing the rest of the population. According to the Congressional Budget Office, the average real after-tax household income of the top 1 percent rose 275 percent from 1979 to 2007. Meanwhile, income for the remainder of the top quintile (81st to 99th percentile) grew 65 percent. Income for the majority of the population in the middle of the scale (21st through 80th percentiles) grew just 37 percent for the same period. And the bottom quintile experienced the least growth income at just 18 percent.

Furthermore, in 1965, a typical corporate CEO [chief executive officer] earned more than twenty times a typical worker; by 2011, the ratio was 383:1, according to the Economic Policy Institute.

While many of the suspected drivers of rising income inequality—globalization, technological change and the rising value of education—affect other nations as well, few have seen as stark a rise in inequality. From 1968 to 2010, the share of national income earned by the top 20 percent rose from 42.6 to 50.2 percent, with gains concentrated at the very top. Meanwhile, the "middle class," the middle 60 percent, saw its share decline from 53.2 to 46.5 percent. This increasing income inequality is captured by the steady rise in the U.S. Gini coefficient, from 0.316 in the mid-1970s to 0.378 in the late 2000s. Today, the U.S. income distribution is one of the most uneven among major developed nations.

Globalization and De-Unionization

Economic forces underlie the growth of income inequality. Highly skilled workers have greatly benefited from worldwide opportunities, from the star actor whose movies reach a global audience to the entrepreneur who can quickly and cheaply bring a new product to market through Chinese contract manufacturing.

Meanwhile, globalization has brought tough competition to other American workers who have seen jobs move overseas, wages stagnate, and unions decline. The median union member earns roughly a quarter more than a nonunion counterpart. Forty years ago, a quarter of private sector workers were represented by unions, but today it is only 6.9 percent. Despite a workforce one-fifth of the size, the public sector has more union members.

Immigration likely plays a role in stagnant wages, especially among workers without a high school degree, of which immigrants make up about half. One study found that a 10 percent increase in the local immigrant population correlated with a 1.3 percent decline in the price of labor-intensive services, but it is difficult to disentangle this competitive effect from others on the labor market.

A noted free trade advocate, Alan Blinder, said that while beneficial for the United States as a whole, the increased labor competition from globalization will be painful for many Americans. He advocated for helping displaced workers through a stronger safety net, reforming education, and encouraging innovation and entrepreneurship. Fellow Princeton economist Paul Krugman believes that "we need to restore the bargaining power that labor has lost over the last thirty years, so that ordinary workers as well as superstars have the power to bargain for good wages."

Education and Technological Change

Most high wages come from high-skill jobs that require a commensurate level of education. After decades of gradually narrowing, the college wage premium has grown dramatically since 1980, as the annual growth in the college educated workforce (2 percent) failed to keep pace with rising demand (3.27 to 3.66 percent) driven by technological change. In 2011, the median earnings of a worker with a bachelor's degree were 65 percent higher than a high school graduate's; holders of professional degrees (MD, JD, MBA [doctor of medicine, doctor of law, and master of business administration, respectively]) enjoyed a 161 percent premium. Higher educational attainment correlates both with higher earnings and lower unemployment.

However, college degrees do not guarantee good jobs. Falling communication and computer costs are leading to the offshoring and automation of some jobs that were once the purview of well-paid professionals, from scientists in pharmaceutical labs to finance and accounting jobs. There is a widening wage premium between those with advanced degrees and those with a bachelor's degree only. Since the 2000s, the wage premium for those with only a four-year degree has remained flat, while for those with advanced degrees it has continued to grow.

Gary S. Becker and Kevin M. Murphy of the University of Chicago see education as the major driver of rising income inequality. "In the United States, the rise in inequality accompanied a rise in the payoff to education and other skills. We believe that the rise in returns on investments in human capital is beneficial and desirable, and policies designed to deal with inequality must take account of its cause." To address income inequality, they argue for policies that would increase the percentages of American youth who complete high school and college, and against making the tax code more progressive.

In a recent survey, 80 percent of economic experts agreed that a leading reason for rising U.S. income inequality was that technological change has affected workers with some skill sets differently than others, but not all prominent economists agree. James K. Galbraith believes that "the skills bias argument—the notion that inequality is being driven by technological change and education and the supply of skills—is comprehensively rebutted by the evidence." He argues instead that the credit cycle has concentrated income in specific sectors, such as finance, tech and real estate.

Income Tax Rates

One tool for addressing income inequality is a more progressive tax code. While some argue that shifting some money from the rich to the poor means that money can be used to create more social utility—the economic concept of declining marginal utility—others see this shift as unfair and unwise because it reduces the ability of more productive citizens to reinvest in the skills and businesses responsible for their higher relative income, thus retarding overall growth. While economic models and theories can attempt to quantify the relationship between inequality and growth, the optimum balance cannot be empirically determined.

The United States has generally cut top income tax rates over the past half century. When John F. Kennedy entered the White House in 1961, the top ordinary income tax bracket—applied to wages and savings interest—was more than 90 percent. Ronald Reagan slashed the top rate from 70 percent in 1981 to 28 percent after 1986. Tax increases under the first President [George H.W.] Bush and President [Bill] Clinton brought the top rate to 39.6 percent, but tax cuts signed by President George W. Bush and reauthorized by President [Barack] Obama set it to 35 percent.

Tax rates on investment income in the form of capital gains taxes and dividends have also declined, with the current rate of 15 percent the lowest since 1933. Investment income ultimately is derived from the after-tax profits of corporations, whose tax rate has also declined since the [Dwight D.] Eisenhower era, from more than 50 percent to today's marginal rate of 35 percent. Corporate income tax has declined steadily as a share both of corporate profits and as a percentage of GDP [gross domestic product] over the past half century.

The Social Security payroll tax, which funds both old-age pensions and Medicare, is regressive because it is a flat rate that only applies to the first $110,100 of wages, in 2012. On the other hand, roughly half of U.S. taxpayers pay no additional federal income tax.

A Tax Policy Center analysis of all federal taxes found overall progressive taxation, with each quartile paying a successively higher rate and the top 0.1 percent paying an effective rate of 30.4 percent. While higher than the 14.1 percent borne by the middle quartile, 30.4 percent is lower than the historical rates paid by this small group, which is earning its largest share of national income since the Great Depression.

Social Program Support

The poverty rate tends to generally follow the economic cycle. As the economy reached new heights in 2000, the poverty rate fell to 11.1 percent—a rate not seen since 1973—but in 2010 the poverty rate had jumped back up to 15.1 percent.

Under President Lyndon Johnson's Great Society [referring to his legislative program of national reform], most assistance was in the form of cash benefits to needy families. Through the 1970s and 1980s, non-cash benefit programs were created or accelerated, including college grants, food stamps, and housing assistance. The 1990s ushered in welfare reform, replacing federal cash assistance with TANF [Temporary Assistance for Needy Families] block grant to states, with work requirements and time limits. The refundable earned income tax credit (created in 1975) was greatly expanded at this time, providing extra cash to workers in an effort to "make work pay."

Today, record numbers receive food stamps, though one in five Americans struggle to afford food. The number of Social Security Disability Insurance recipients has surged by more than 22 percent since the recession began, as that program effectively acts as a long-term unemployment benefit for some.

From Medicaid to unemployment benefits, many social support programs are driven by decisions at the state level. States have less flexibility to run deficits and many have cut programs to needy citizens. Pennsylvania recently joined other states in eliminating its general assistance program. One caseworker observed: "My clients have lost an important source of funds for life's necessities, while they face longer wait lists for job training programs."

A longer term source of income disparity is strengthening: It is increasingly difficult to reach a higher economic status than your parents. Many Americans take pride in the belief that everyone has a chance to "make it big" and rags-to-riches stories are almost legends. But today, more than 40 percent of those born into the lowest income quintile will stay there, and less than 30 percent will make an above-average income.

Among developed countries, only the United Kingdom has less class mobility; in 2006, the Brookings Institution found that 47 percent of U.S. parents' income advantages are passed to their children, greater than in France (41 percent), Germany (32 percent) or Sweden (27 percent). The countries with the highest mobility were Canada, Norway, Finland and Denmark, where less than 20 percent of economic disadvantages are passed to children.

The Political Impact of Economic Inequality

The growing gap between the rich and poor may exacerbate political disunity. Economist Joseph E. Stiglitz of Columbia University examined this in his recent book, *The Price of Inequality*, and argued that no one has an interest in stark inequality. "The rich do not exist in a vacuum. They need a functioning society around them to sustain their position. Widely unequal societies do not function efficiently and their economies are neither stable nor sustainable."

The Pew Research Center found increasing anxiety among America's middle class, with 85 percent expressing greater difficulty in maintaining their standard of living. While a majority of Americans see income inequality as a big problem, polls also show more desire for economic growth and greater equality of opportunity.

During the debate in late 2010 over whether to extend the Bush-era tax rates, influential behavioral economist Richard H. Thaler asked "whether we want a society in which the rich take an ever-increasing share of the pie, or prefer to return to conditions that allow all classes to anticipate an increasing standard of living." The former chairman of Bush's Council of Economic Advisers, N. Gregory Mankiw, argued that raising his marginal tax rate would lead him—and many others—to work less. This tension between equality and growth is likely to remain unresolved for the foreseeable future.

Finally, an August 2012 paper by the Hoover Institution of Stanford [University] argued that income inequality is not rising. Their analysis considered after-tax income and added in non-cash benefits from employers and government programs, and calculated a decline in the U.S. Gini coefficient from 1993 to 2009. The authors argued that reducing income inequality would not improve economic well-being, and policy makers should instead target opportunity inequality.

New Civil War Erupts, Led by Super Rich, GOP

Paul B. Farrell

Paul B. Farrell is an investing and personal finance columnist for MarketWatch as well as other online media. He is also a television commentator and the author of four books, including The Millionaire Code: 16 Paths to Wealth Building.

The warfare between the classes is being waged and won by the rich, who exploit crises for their own personal gain, warns Farrell in the following viewpoint. He summarizes a Republican strategy of "disaster capitalism," which he describes as creating a crisis, then demanding that the way out of the crisis is to give state governments dictatorial powers. Republican governors will then use these powers to privatize government, decimate social programs, and enrich their already rich cronies, Farrell cautions.

Yes, "there's class warfare, all right," warns [businessman and investor] Warren Buffett. "But it's my class, the rich class, that's making war, and we're winning." Yes, the rich are making war against us. And yes, they are winning. Why? Because so many are fighting this new American Civil War between the rich and the rest.

Not just the 16 new GOP [Republican] governors in Wisconsin, Michigan, Ohio, Florida, and across America fighting for new powers. Others include: Chamber of Commerce billionaires, Koch brothers [David and Charles Koch], Forbes 400, Karl Rove's American Crossroads, Grover Norquist's Americans for Tax Reform—which now has 97% of House Republicans and 85% of the GOP senators signed on his "no new taxes" pledge—the Tea Party [a conservative political movement] and Reaganomics [economic policies named for Ronald Reagan] ideologues.

Wake up America. You are under attack. Stop kidding yourself. We are at war. In fact, we have been fighting this Civil War for a generation, since Ronald Reagan was elected in 1981. Recently Buffett renewed the battle cry: The "rich class" is winning this war. Except most Americans still don't realize they're losing, don't see the prize at stake.

All this was predicted back in September 2008 by Naomi Klein, author of *Shock Doctrine: The Rise of Disaster Capitalism*. Yes, we were warned that the GOP's Reaganomics ideology would stage a rapid comeback . . . warned before the market collapsed . . . before Wall Street was virtually bankrupt . . . before Treasury Secretary Henry Paulson conned Congress into $787 billion in bailouts . . . warned before [Barack] Obama's 2008 election.

Free Market Reaganomics Roaring Back, More Powerful than Before

Yes, back in the heat of battle, in September 2008, Klein warned America: "Whatever the events of this week mean, nobody should believe the overblown claims that the market crisis signals the death of 'free market' ideology." Then the meltdown went nuclear.

Klein warned: "Free market ideology has always been a servant to the interests of capital, and its presence ebbs and flows depending on its usefulness to those interests. During boom times, it's profitable to preach laissez-faire [doctrine calling for little government regulation of commerce] because an absentee government allows speculative bubbles to inflate."

But "when those bubbles burst, the ideology becomes a hindrance, and it goes dormant while big government rides to the rescue." Remember: A week later Paulson was on his knee, begging House Speaker Nancy Pelosi for that $787 billion

Protesters rally together outside the office of US senator Marco Rubio (R-FL) on December 10, 2012, in Doral, Florida. The protesters are hoping that senators like Rubio will not cut Medicare or Social Security benefits and will agree to raise taxes on the top 2 percent of earners in the United States. © Joe Raedle/Getty Image News/Getty Images.

bailout, to save our incompetent Wall Street banks that caused the meltdown from certain bankruptcy.

"But rest assured," continued Klein in September 2008, Reaganomics "ideology will come roaring back when the bailouts are done. The massive debts the public is accumulating to bail out the speculators will then become part of a global budget crisis that will be the rationalization for deep cuts to social programs, and for a renewed push to privatize."

And yes, America, this war strategy is happening thanks to General Buffett, the new GOP Congress and 16 aggressive anti-democracy GOP governors.

Escalation of New Civil War: GOP Dictators Killing Democracy

After the 2010 election of these new GOP governors, the new Civil War escalated with a new phase of self-destructive "disaster capitalism," thanks to the Supreme Court's *Citizens United* decision [a decision allowing independent political expenditures by corporations and unions]. Their strategy was first revealed in the Wisconsin dictator Scott Walker's war against the unions. Then last week [the week of March 13, 2011] the GOP assault went nuclear.

Michigan's GOP Gov. Rick Snyder signed the "much despised emergency financial manager legislation into law," said local ABC news, labeling the law "draconic" for giving the governor new dictatorial powers to appoint "emergency financial managers ... to run struggling cities and schools, including the ability to terminate union contracts."

We learned of Snyder's democracy-killing coup a week earlier when MSNBC's Rachel Maddow interviewed Naomi Klein. Maddow also exposed another particularly harsh tactic: Snyder's $1.7 billion tax hikes against seniors and the poor. He was "not using it to close the budget gap. He is giving it away in the form of $1.8 billion in corporate tax cuts."

Get it, folks? In the GOP governors' new strategy escalating this Civil War, the GOP is robbing the poor to give to the rich.

Maddow exposed the truth behind the GOP's economic strategy: "It's not about the budget in Michigan ... not about the budget in Wisconsin ... not about the budget in Florida ... not about the budget in Ohio ... what Michiganders have been trying to get the rest of the country to pay attention to is that what these Republicans are doing in the states is not just not about the budget. It's about something far worse." Wake up America.

GOP Using "Shock Doctrine" to Gain New Anti-Democracy Powers

The GOP is anti-democracy: With the GOP, "this whole democracy thing" is "very inefficient," warned Klein. Republican governors are using "a fiscal crisis as a pretext to do stuff they otherwise want to do. ... Republicans in Michigan want to be able to unilaterally abolish your town. And how do you know when you're in a financial emergency? Because the governor tells you . . . or a company he hires."

Yes the GOP, the party of big business and billionaires, secretly hates democracy, it's too inefficient for the rich class.

In the interview, Klein reiterated: The GOP governors' strategy is a clear example of "disaster capitalism," the Reaganomics war strategy that has dominated, obsessed and driven the GOP for a generation. Klein warns, "these guys have been at this for 30 years," it is "an ideological movement . . . they believe in a whole bunch of stuff that's not very popular," like "privatizing the local water system, busting unions, privatizing entire towns. If they said all this in an election they'd lose."

And that's why crises are so crucial to the GOP war strategies to take over America: Crises "are very, very handy, because you can say we have no choice. . . . The sky is falling in." Then the GOP governors "can consolidate power. We remember this from the Bush administration. They did this at the federal level. After 9/11 [referring to the September 11, 2001, terrorist attacks on the United States], they said, we have a crisis, and we have to essentially rule by fiat."

But the truth, warns Klein, is that the GOP "really doesn't believe in the governments that they are running . . . this is a really old story." The greed of their billionaire backers is insatiable. They do not like democracy. And the actions of the new GOP governors is proof that what they really want are dictatorial powers to privatize government and get personally richer.

GOP Megalomania: Create Crises, Change the Course of History

Money, power, greed: That's why the GOP is "so desperate to tie the hands of unions. Why 16 states are facing similar battles" says Klein, because "unions are the final line of defense against privatization of the public sector. Unions are the ones who fight privatization of the school system, of the water system, of the power system."

And that's why, in this new American Civil War the GOP keeps its "eye on the prize, because there's a lot of money to be made in the kinds of crony deals that could be rammed through when you have all of that power consolidated in the governor's office." Get it?

Remember when Wisconsin dictator Scott Walker thought he was talking to billionaire GOP backer David Koch: The vision of the GOP became very clear. Walker said: "This is our moment to change the course of history." This same egomaniacal mind-set has obsessed the GOP since Reaganomics emerged a generation ago. Crises are opportunities for the GOP, whether real or fake (as we saw in Wisconsin and Iraq), every crisis is an excuse for the GOP's dictators to activate every possible weapon in their "disaster capitalism" arsenal.

Yes, each crisis triggers a grandiose button in the GOP psyche, an obsession to "change the course of history," to act like Ronald Reagan in the "moment that ended communism," as Walker said. That's also why GOP governors like Walker are comparing the unions to communism, drawing clear battle lines in this new American "Civil War."

"Disaster Capitalism" Is the GOP Strategy in This New Civil War

In my review of *The Shock Doctrine: The Rise of Disaster Capitalism* a few years ago I called it "the most important book on economics in the 21st century." That's truer today. Events of the past four years make this a must-read for anyone interested in understanding the Second American Civil War being fought by Buffett's rich class, Wall Street CEOs [chief executive officers] and the GOP dictators battling to dominate America.

Reaganomics, "shock doctrine" and disaster capitalism all define the same ideology that's been driving the GOP for over a generation, an ideology gaining even more power now as they accelerate their battle plans, increasing efforts to gain total power over our government, economy and culture, a strategy that will ultimately destroy everything.

Klein's recent interview with Maddow exposed the GOP's charade: Now we know with certainty that the budget crises in the 50 states were "created on Wall Street then moved to Main Street, deepened by the policy decisions to bail out banks instead of bailing out homeowners, instead of bailing out workers. And that means your tax base collapses."

We know Wall Street greed was the fuel igniting America's current economic problems. And now, unfortunately, average Americans have "to pay for the crisis again. First, with a bailout. And now, people are paying with it again, with budget cuts."

And underneath it all is the GOP's free market Reaganomics ideology. Wake up America, you're losing the new Civil War to a rich class that's lost its moral compass.

Bottom line, Klein warns: "What this fight is really about is not unions versus taxpayers. . . . It's a fight about who's going to pay for the crisis that was created by the wealthiest elite in this country."

Actually, it's even worse. Because while we averted total collapse, it was only delayed, destined to return soon and finally overwhelm America. Remember Uncle Warren's battle cry: "The rich class is winning."

The Real Class Conflict Is Between Taxpayers and Tax Consumers

Steve Bartin

Steve Bartin is the editor and publisher of Newsalert, Overpaid Government Worker, *and* Newsfeed Alert, *and a contributing editor to NewGeography.com.*

The real class conflict in America is between taxpayers and government workers, argues Bartin in the following viewpoint. The welfare state in America was created when in the early twentieth century John Dewey and other intellectuals encouraged the growth of the public sector, Bartin contends. Government workers will continue to vote for politicians who support the welfare state that pays their lucrative salaries, he maintains.

Lately, there's been much talk about the generous compensation of government workers. This is understandable after a long recession in which many private sector workers got laid off or took cuts in compensation levels. As *USA Today* reminds us, federal pay has surpassed private sector wages. Since private sector workers pay the taxes that fund government workers' wages, conflict exists.

Marxists have long stated that class conflict exists between workers and the owners of capital. [Karl] Marx and his followers were wrong about that. Class conflict exists between taxpayers and tax consumers. As the nearly forgotten nineteenth-century politician John C. Calhoun stated:

> The necessary result, then, of the unequal fiscal action of the government is, to divide the community into two great

classes; one consisting of those who, in reality, pay the taxes, and, of course, bear exclusively the burthen of supporting the government; and the other, of those who are the recipients of their proceeds, through disbursements, and who are, in fact, supported by the government; or, in fewer words, to divide it into taxpayers and tax consumers.

But the effect of this is to place them in antagonistic relations in reference to the fiscal action of the government and the entire course of policy therewith connected. For the greater the taxes and disbursements, the greater the gain of the one and the loss of the other—and vice versa. Consequently, the more the policy of the government is calculated to increase taxes and disbursements, the more it will be favored by the one and opposed by the other.

Calhoun's line of thinking is simply ignored by university intellectuals and the liberal mainstream press. Calhoun's libertarian class analysis has survived in the last several decades by libertarian economists Murray Rothbard and Hans-Hermann Hoppe. To libertarians like Rothbard and Hoppe, private sector workers earn their wages through satisfying consumer wants by means of voluntary cooperation in the marketplace. The public sector earns their compensation through theft by majority-rule democracy, the political means. Theft through majority voting is highly effective when government workers are given the right to vote.

The results have been rather lucrative. Why else would public schoolteachers be so involved in America's political process? But teachers aren't the only rent seekers. Ten percent of Massachusetts state troopers make more than their governor. Over 3,600 California prison guards make over $100,000 a year. Madison, Wisconsin's highest paid government worker is a bus driver making $159,258 a year.

To get the welfare state off the radar in America, an ideology was needed to push on the public. Before 1913, there wasn't much of a welfare state in America. Without a central bank and an income tax, the ability to finance an activist government was virtually impossible. John Dewey and other intellectuals, in early twentieth-century America, promoted a vision of an increasing public sector based on cooperation and altruism unencumbered by the profit motive. This mind-set would have us believe that those who don't work for an institution based on a quarterly profit basis are "public spirited."

Public choice economists James Buchanan and Gordon Tullock have pointed out that self-interest doesn't disappear in the political process:

> [A] significant factor in the popular support for socialism through the centuries has been the underlying faith that the shift of an activity from the realm of private to that of social choice involves the replacement of the motive of private gain by that of social good. Throughout the ages the profit-seeker, the utility-maximizer, has found few friends among the moral and the political philosophers. In the last two centuries the pursuit of private gain has been tolerated begrudgingly in the private sector, with the alleged "exploitation" always carefully mentioned in passing. In the political sphere the pursuit of private gain by the individual participant has been almost universally condemned as "evil" by moral philosophers of many shades. No one seems to have explored carefully the implicit assumption that the individual must somehow shift his psychological and moral gears when he moves between the private and the social aspects of life.

Government workers are reliable voters for politicians that will vote for higher taxes and more government spending. The great nineteenth-century libertarian thinker Herbert Spencer predicted what socialism and the welfare state would bring:

> All socialism involves slavery.

> What is essential to the idea of a slave? We primarily think of him as one who is owned by another. To be more than

nominal, however, the ownership must be shown by control of the slave's actions—a control which is habitually for the benefit of the controller. That which fundamentally distinguishes the slave is that he labours under coercion to satisfy another's desires. The relation admits of sundry gradations. Remembering that originally the slave is a prisoner whose life is at the mercy of his captor, it suffices here to note that there is a harsh form of slavery in which, treated as an animal, he has to expend his entire effort for his owner's advantage.

In modern-day America, some state governments already exhibit disturbing elements of slavery. The state constitutions of New York and Illinois clearly state that government workers' pensions can't be diminished. Thus, taxpayers are responsible for generous compensation that they will not get but are coerced into paying. Historically, the purpose of a constitution is to enumerate and limit the power of government, not to enshrine special privileges for a special class of individuals.

In the coming years, the war between those who pay taxes and those who receive them will only increase. It could be college students who feel they are entitled to pay tuitions cheaper than grammar school tuitions or government workers who can retire at 42 instead of 65. Taxation without representation has long been a powerful rallying cry in America. In the near future, we may be hearing a derivative of that famous slogan: no representation without taxation. Many are beginning to question whether low taxes are possible with government workers allowed to vote.

The Real Class War
Is Between the Old and
the Young

Nick Gillespie

*Nick Gillespie is the editor in chief of Reason.com and Reason
TV, as well as the coauthor with Matt Welch of* The Declaration
of Independents: How Libertarian Politics Can Fix What's
Wrong with America.

*The real class warfare in America is between the old and the
young, maintains Gillespie in the following viewpoint. The only
group whose net worth increased from 1984 to 2009 was that of
people fifty-five years of age or older, he points out. Government
policy favors the old over the young, with the young being forced
to pay an inordinate share to maintain the relatively affluent
lifestyle of seniors, Gillespie complains.*

Hey kids, wake up! Stop playing your Xbox while listening
to your Facebooks on the iPod and wearing your iPad
with the cap turned backwards with the droopy pants and the
bikini underwear listening to Snoopy Poopy Poop Dogg and
the Enema Man and all that!

Take a break from getting yet another tattoo on your ass
bone or your nipples pierced already! And STFU [shut up]
about the 1 Percent vs. the 99 Percent!

You're not getting screwed by billionaires and plutocrats.
You're getting screwed by Mom and Dad.

Systematically and in all sorts of ways. Old people are doing everything possible to rob you of your money, your future, your dignity, and your freedom.

Here's the irony, too (in a sort of Alanis Morissette [Canadian American singer/songwriter] sense): You're getting hosed by the very same group that 45 years ago was bitching and moaning about "the generation gap" and how their parents just didn't understand what really mattered in life.

Hence, many of the early pop anthems of the baby boomers—technically, those born between 1946 and 1964 but for all intents and purposes folks 55 years and older—focused on how stupid old people were ("don't criticize what you can't understand") and how young people would rather croak themselves then end up like their parents ("I hope I die before I get old"). "We are stardust, we are golden," sang Crosby, Stills, Nash and Young [a folk/rock group] at Woodstock. "We got to get ourselves back to the garden." Flash forward four or five decades, a couple of hundred pounds, the odd organ transplant, random arrests and jail stints, and the only garden David Crosby is getting back to is the Olive Garden with its unlimited pasta bowls and breadsticks. What small parts of American life and power the boomers don't yet run they will soon enough.

Did you read that *New York Times* op-ed that called for a brand-spankin' new military draft and national service plan? "Let's Draft Our Kids," by veteran (read: old, born in 1955) journalist Thomas Ricks, is symptomatic of the new vibe, a kind of reverse *Logan's Run* scenario. In that god-awful 1976 flick, when you turned 30, you were killed for the common good. Nowadays, it's more like life begins at 30. Which is confusing because 40 is the new 30 and 50 is the new 40 and on and on. The important thing: Youth is no longer to be wasted on the young.

Ricks suggests letting high school grads pick from either 18 months of military service or two years of civilian service, in return for free college tuition and subsidized health care and mortgages (libertarians, he notes, could opt out of service by forfeiting benefits though apparently not avoiding taxes).

Beyond all the obviously great and good and wonderful things that come of forced labor, Ricks suggests that "having a draft might . . . make Americans think more carefully before going to war." Sure it would. Just like it did in the past when we actually had a draft.

Expect this sort of plan to get more and more respectful hearings if unemployment stays high for another few weeks. Or as former hippies and punks get up there in years. Last year [in 2011], during an appearance I had on *Real Time with Bill Maher*, the host and other guests (all of us well north of 30) thought mandatory service was a fine notion. Back in the 1980s and '90s, national service was a pet project of folks such as Sen. Bill Bradley (D-N.J.) and right-wing icon Bill Buckley [William F. Buckley Jr.] (who wrote a book, *Gratitude*, on the topic).

Oddly, back in the actual 1960s, one of the few things that hippies and [Republican politicians] Barry Goldwater and Ronald Reagan could all agree on was that conscription was a really bad thing. For god's sake, Richard Nixon created a commission to end the draft. But that was then, and this is now.

And right now, old people are not going gentle into that good night. They know they're going to need younger people to change their diapers and pay their bills for them, literally and figuratively. As Hillary Clinton put it in 1999, nobody's going to do that if they have any option not to. Speaking to a National Education Association meeting, she explained one of the great benefits of old-age entitlements was that they meant you didn't have to live with your goddamn parents.

"In a very real sense," she said, "Medicare and Social Security say to our older people: We're going to help you remain independent. . . . We're going to free up the resources that might otherwise have to come directly to you from your family, so that they can do what you did—raise the next generation, send their children to college, hold down the jobs that enable them to move forward."

You got that? The author of *It Takes a Village*, a paean to the intricate bonds across and among generations, thinks one of the great selling points of Social Security is that it means you don't have to make room for granddaddy. Goddammit, we need that room for a home office! "There would be many families who would have to choose between supporting a parent—an elderly parent—and sending a child to college." She mused, "That would cause a lot of difficult decisions in our lives, wouldn't it?" Yes, it would, so it makes sense to give old people enough of other people's money so you don't have to see them except on holidays.

As a point of fact, retirees aren't particularly "independent" if they rely on tax dollars for income, are they? But here's the real rub, kids: You're getting screwed by Social Security, a program that is now more sacrosanct to aging boomers than *Sgt. Pepper's Lonely Hearts Club Band* [a 1967 album from the rock band the Beatles]. You're paying more into the system than you're ever going to get out. No wonder it's mandatory. C. Eugene Steuerle and Stephanie Rennane put out a study for the Urban Institute last summer that should have caused far more riots than anything that happened at Zuccotti Park [a park in New York City where Occupy Wall Street protesters demonstrated]. They document that folks making average wages who retired in 2010 will get a raw deal over the coming decades. The deal will only get worse if you retire in, say, 2030. Read it and weep, kids, and don't believe it when old people who are either already on Social Security or about to join that club tell you it's part of a generational bargain that can't be changed even if retirees are totally wealthy compared to you.

Indeed, be wary of folks telling you that means-testing old-age entitlements is insulting and un-American. Because the fact of the matter is that between 1984 and 2009, the only households that did well are those headed by people 55 years or older. Fact is, you're coughing up 12.4 percent of your compensation for a system that will give you less money than you gave it. And that's assuming the system is still around in recognizable form when you're ready for retirement. On top of that negative return, expect to read more articles like this one by *Spy* [magazine] co-creator Kurt Andersen (b. 1954) in which the one-time snark-meister bemoans the fact that the 1960s made us "all shamelessly selfish." Huh? Who's *we*, kemo sabe ["trusty scout," from *The Lone Ranger*]? Those of us either too young or too unborn to remember the '60s aren't being selfish if we call attention to a system that loots the relatively young and relatively poor to give money to the relatively old and relatively rich. We're being fair.

So kiddos, you're getting screwed by old people who expect you to maintain a system that benefits them at your expense, regardless of their needs or yours. Thanks, Mom and Dad! And we just might be in the early stages of a bring-back-the-draft movement, where you would get to choose between painting military barracks for 18 months or sharpening a teacher's pencils for two years.

Then chew on this: One of the primary ways that President [Barack] Obama (born 1961) is making the so-called [Patient Protection and] Affordable Care Act affordable is by having you foot more than your share of the bill.

Think it through for a moment, especially given that younger voters seem to really dig him. The younger you are, the less likely you are to need health care, much less insurance (there is a difference). The smart move for most generally healthy younger people is to take out a catastrophic coverage plan that would cover you in the event of a big accident. Thanks to Obamacare, you've got to get covered, either by your parents' plan or otherwise. The predictable result is that plans for younger people are getting more expensive precisely at the moment they are required by law (finally, a case where correlation meets causation!). That all plans are going to have

to conform to higher-than-before benefit schedules ain't helping things either. Some colleges are dropping student plans as
a result.

And just wait until those price-capped government-run
health-care exchanges finally get set up. By law, the exchanges
can't charge their oldest beneficiaries more than three times
what they charge their youngest beneficiaries. That's despite
the actuarial reality that the older group costs insurers six
times as much. So you're helping balance the books there, too.
Welcome to community rating, kids.

Another way you're helping balance the books: It'll be
your future earnings that will pay the taxes to cover the massive amount of debt that local, state, and federal governments
have rung up over the past few decades. Even before the Great
Recession, the feds were spending like a drunken sailor (no
disrespect to drunken sailors). Nowadays, the feds are borrow-
ing something like 40 cents of every dollar they're spending.
That bill is going to come due eventually and when it does,
the people who spent it will be long dead. And so will the
economy, suffering from a "debt hangover" that all the Advil
in the world won't help. We're getting perilously close to the
debt-to-GDP [gross domestic product] ratios that economists
Carmen M. Reinhart, Vincent R. Reinhart, and Kenneth Rogoff
say will significantly retard economic growth for an average of
23 years.

It should go without saying that it doesn't have to be this
way. And don't buy into the idea that the way things are is
just part of the circle of life. You're the mark here, the chump
who's believing in Bernie Madoff [an investment adviser who
swindled his clients in a fraudulent investment operation]
even after the grift has been revealed. There's not going to be
a bigger idiot to come along and keep the pyramid scheme
alive. You can tell yourself that this is all part of living in a society, that it's for the common good, that there's simply no
way a class of people with only 45 times the amount of house-

hold income as you do can get by without you sacrificing so much. But you're kidding yourself, kiddo.

More to the point: Older generations don't need to mop up all the gravy from their kids' bowls. Those of them who can afford to should pay their own way and, in a generational exchange observed for hundreds of generations, could even leave things for their heirs (this is impossible with Social Security, of course). The days when being old universally meant being poor or sick are thankfully behind us and old-age entitlements should change to reflect that reality. We can help the truly needy among us without creating a system in which young people's already small incomes and savings are reduced further to prop up the relatively plush living standards of older Americans. . . . The young shouldn't be sacrificed to the real and imagined needs of the old.

The one thing I know for damn sure as a parent and a late-era boomer (b. 1963) is that I would never want to charge my existence onto my kids' credit card. If that means we need to start living within our means as a society, that's not really a tough call, is it?

For Further Discussion

1. In chapter 1, George H. Ford writes that to create great literature, a writer needs to have extraordinary personal experiences on which to draw. What experiences from Dickens's life might he have used to write *A Tale of Two Cities? Explain.*

2. Critics John Gross and Cates Baldridge present opposing views on Dickens's opinion on individualism. Gross believes that Dickens feared the unruly crowd even though he celebrated the sacrifice of the common people. Baldridge suggests that Dickens was deeply frustrated with the acquisitive, individualistic society of Victorian England and sympathetic to the revolutionaries. Which critic do you agree with, and why?

3. In chapter 2, critic Nicholas Rance points out some of the similarities between prerevolutionary France and Victorian England. What are some of these similarities, and what are some of the differences discussed?

4. In chapter 3, commentators David Schultz and Kip Hagopian and Lee Ohanian have differing opinions on income inequality in America. Schultz argues that income inequality is a serious issue, whereas Hagopian and Ohanian contend it is not a serious problem. Which argument do you support, and why?

For Further Reading

Charlotte Brontë, *Villette*. Leipzig, Germany: B. Tauchnitz, 1853.

Thomas Carlyle, *The French Revolution: A History*. London: Chapman & Hall, 1837.

Charles Dickens, *Barnaby Rudge: A Tale of the Riots of 'Eighty*. London: Chapman & Hall, 1841.

————, *Bleak House*. London: Bradbury and Evans, 1853.

————, *The Life and Adventures of Nicholas Nickleby*. London: Chapman & Hall, 1839.

————, *Little Dorrit*. London: Bradbury and Evans, 1857.

————, *Our Mutual Friend*. London: Chapman & Hall, 1865.

Alexandre Dumas, *The Three Musketeers*. London: Horace Marshall & Son, 1844.

George Eliot, *Silas Marner: The Weaver of Raveloe*. Edinburgh, Scotland: W. Blackwood and Sons, 1861.

Thomas Hardy, *Tess of the D'Urbervilles: A Pure Woman Faithfully Presented*. London: Harper & Brothers, 1891.

Victor Hugo, *Les Misérables*. Paris: Pagnerre, 1862.

Emmuska Orczy, *The Scarlet Pimpernel*. London: Hutchinson & Co., 1905.

Leo Tolstoy, *War and Peace*. St. Petersburg, Russia: Russkiy Vestnik, 1869.

Anthony Trollope, *The Three Clerks*. London: Richard Bentley, 1857.

Bibliography

Books

Charles E.   *Twentieth Century Interpretations of A*
Beckwith, ed.   *Tale of Two Cities; A Collection of*
                    Critical Essays. Englewood Cliffs, NJ:
                    Prentice-Hall, 1972.

Berch Berberoglu   *Class and Class Conflict in the Age of*
                    Globalization. Lanham, MD:
                    Lexington Books, 2009.

Philip Collins, ed. *Dickens: The Critical Heritage.*
                    London: Routledge & Kegan Paul,
                    1971.

Ralph W.V. Elliott *A Critical Commentary of Dickens's A*
                    Tale of Two Cities. London:
                    Macmillan, 1966.

John Forster   *The Life of Charles Dickens.* Ed. Holly
                    Furneaux. New York: Sterling
                    Signature, 2011.

Ruth Glancy   *A Tale of Two Cities: Dickens's*
                    Revolutionary Novel. Boston: Twayne
                    Publishers, 1991.

Barbara Hardy   *The Moral Art of Dickens.* New York:
                    Oxford University Press, 1970.

Edgar Johnson   *Charles Dickens, His Tragedy and*
                    Triumph. New York: Penguin, 1979.

F.R. Leavis and   *Dickens the Novelist.* New Brunswick,
Q.D. Leavis   NJ: Rutgers University Press, 1979.

Gregory C. Leavitt	*Class Conflict: The Pursuit and History of American Justice.* New Brunswick, NJ: Transaction Publishers, 2013.
Norman MacKenzie and Jeanne MacKenzie	*Dickens: A Life.* New York: Oxford University Press, 1979.
Harlan S. Nelson	*Charles Dickens.* Boston: Twayne, 1981.
William Oddie	*Dickens and Carlyle: The Question of Influence.* London: Centenary Press, 1972.
Andrew Sanders	*The Victorian Historical Novel, 1840–1880.* New York: St. Martin's Press, 1979.
Jane Smiley	*Charles Dickens.* New York: Viking, 2002.
Alexander Welsh	*The City of Dickens.* Cambridge, MA: Harvard University Press, 1986.
Angus Wilson	*The World of Charles Dickens.* London: Secker & Warburg, 1970.

Periodicals and Internet Sources

Robert Alter	"The Demons of History in Dickens' Tale," *Novel: A Forum on Fiction,* vol. 2, no. 2, Winter 1969, pp. 135–142.
Dorothy Sue Cobble	"Don't Blame the Workers," *Dissent,* vol. 59, no. 1, Winter 2012, pp. 35–39.

Terry Eagleton   "Contradictory Dickens," *Red Pepper*, February 2012.

Edwin M. Eigner   "Charles Darnay and Revolutionary Identity," *Dickens Studies Annual*, vol. 12, 1983, pp. 147–160.

Gareth Stedman Jones   "The Redemptive Power of Violence?: Carlyle, Marx, and Dickens," *History Workshop Journal*, vol. 65, no. 1, Spring 2008, pp. 1–22.

John B. Lamb   "Domesticating History: Revolution and Moral Management in *A Tale of Two Cities*," *Dickens Studies Annual*, vol. 25, 1996, pp. 227–243.

Nicholas Lemann   "Evening the Odds," *New Yorker*, vol. 88, no. 10, April 23, 2012, p. 68.

Teresa Mangum   "Dickens and the Female Terrorist: The Long Shadow of Madame Defarge," *Nineteenth-Century Contexts*, vol. 31, no. 2, June 2009, pp. 143–160.

John P. McWilliams Jr.   "Progress Without Politics: *A Tale of Two Cities*," *CLIO*, vol. 7, no. 1, Fall 1977, pp. 19–31.

Sylvere Monod   "Dickens's Attitudes in *A Tale of Two Cities*," *Nineteenth-Century Fiction*, vol. 24, no. 4, March 1970, pp. 488–505.

William E. Pike   "Was Dickens Really a Socialist?," *Freeman*, vol. 56, no. 10, December 2006.

J.M. Rignall   "Dickens and the Catastrophic Continuum of History in *A Tale of Two Cities*," *ELH*, vol. 51, no. 3, 1984, pp. 575–587.

Knud Sorensen   "Carlyle and Dickens on the French Revolution: A Stylistic Study," *Dolphin*, vol. 19, 1990, pp. 134–145.

G. Robert Stange   "Dickens and the Fiery Past: *A Tale of Two Cities* Reconsidered," *English Journal*, vol. 46, no. 7, October 1957, pp. 381–390.

James Fitzjames Stephen   "Mr. Dickens as a Politician," *Saturday Review*, January 3, 1857, p. 9.

Daniel Stout   "Nothing Personal: The Decapitation of Character in *A Tale of Two Cities*," *Novel: A Forum on Fiction*, vol. 41, no. 1, Fall 2007, pp. 29–52.

Bjorn Tysdahl   "Europe Is Not the Other: *A Tale of Two Cities*," *Dickens Quarterly*, vol. 15, no. 2, June 1998, pp. 111–122.

Maja-Lisa Von Sneidern   "'An Amazingly Good Jackal': Race and Labor in Dickens's *A Tale of Two Cities*," *South Atlantic Review*, vol. 66, no. 2, Spring 2001, pp. 64–90.

Index